# Torture and Truth

First published in 1991, this book — through the examination of ancient Greek literary, philosophical and legal texts — analyses how the Athenian torture of slaves emerged from and reinforced the concept of truth as something hidden in the human body. It discusses the tradition of understanding truth as something that is generally concealed and the ideas of 'secret space' in both the female body and the Greek temple. This philosophy and practice is related to Greek views of the 'Other' (women and outsiders) and considers the role of torture in distinguishing slave and free in ancient Athens. A wide range of perspectives — from Plato to Sartre — are employed to examine the subject.

# Torture and Truth

**Page duBois**

Routledge
Taylor & Francis Group

First published in 1991
by Routledge

This edition first published in 2016 by Routledge
2 Park Square, Milton Park, Abingdon, Oxon, OX14 4RN
and by Routledge
711 Third Avenue, New York, NY 10017

*Routledge is an imprint of the Taylor & Francis Group, an informa business*

**Publisher's Note**
The publisher has gone to great lengths to ensure the quality of this reprint but points out that some imperfections in the original copies may be apparent.

**Disclaimer**
The publisher has made every effort to trace copyright holders and welcomes correspondence from those they have been unable to contact.

A Library of Congress record exists under LC control number: 8949565


ISBN 13: 978-1-138-20362-4 (hbk)
ISBN 13: 978-1-315-47089-4 (ebk)
ISBN 13: 978-1-138-20364-8 (pbk)

# TORTURE
### *and*
# TRUTH

## PAGE duBOIS

ROUTLEDGE

New York • London

Published in 1991 by

Routledge
An imprint of Routledge, Chapman and Hall, Inc.
29 West 35 Street
New York, NY 10001

Published in Great Britain by

Routledge
11 New Fetter Lane
London EC4P 4EE

**Library of Congress Cataloging in Publication Data**

DuBois, Page
    Torture and truth / Page DuBois
       p.    cm.
    Includes bibliographical references.
    ISBN 0-415-90212-6   ISBN 0-415-90213-4 (pbk.)
    1. Torture—Greece—History.  2. Greece—
Civilization—To 146 B.C.
    3. Torture—History.  I. Title
HV8599.G82D83   1990
364.6'7—dc20                      89-49565

**British Library Cataloging in publication data also
available**

For Jean-Pierre Vernant

# Contents

# Contents

# 1

# Rome, 1985

A banner over the Via Nazionale announced the exhibit; it hung there, above the exhaust fumes, the laboring, overcrowded city buses, luxury German buses equipped with refrigerator bars, over tourists' cars and begging gypsy children. *Macchine atroci*, it said, all summer long.

One sweltering summer evening, we went to see. The atrocious machines were set up in the garden of the Quirinal Palace. The Sabines are said to have settled the Quirinal, highest of Rome's seven hills. The name Quirinal is derived either from a temple of Quirinus, a name given to Romulus after his deification, or from the Sabine town Cures; little remains of antiquity there, besides statues of Castor and Pollux, Roman imperial copies of Greek originals of the fifth century B.C.E. Vittoria Colonna met with Michelangelo nearby, in a house next to the church of San Silvestro al Quirinale. The Palazzo del Quirinale was built in stages from 1574 to 1740. The popes once spent the summer in the Quirinal Palace; it is now the residence of the president of the Republic.

The machines sat in the garden—the rack, a sort of chaise longue made of wood, the garrot, a device to encircle the neck and plunge a sharpened metal spike into the throat, a cage suspended from a Quirinal tree, in which condemned prisoners had once been left to starve to death in view of passers-by. I had never known quite what "the rack" was; the caption explained that the prisoner had been literally stretched on it, stretched until the joints gave, so that the body was broken up inside the envelope of the skin.

I gazed uneasily at the others visiting this spot. There were tourists, foreigners and Italians, scattered around the torture implements, and I tried to imagine what brought them there. Was it a historical curiosity about the Middle Ages, or the same desire that brings people to horror movies, or sexual desire invested in bondage and discipline? I was there too.

Inside sat other devices. The iron maiden of Frankfurt, a larger-than-life-size female body, cast in iron, strangely reminiscent of one of those Russian dolls, a rounded maternal peasant body that opens horizontally to reveal another identical doll inside, that opens again and again until one reaches a baby, perhaps, I can't recall, in its deepest inside. This body, propped open, had been cast with a vertical split, its interior consisting of two sets of sharp iron spikes that, when the maiden was closed on a captive human body, penetrated that body, trapping it upright as it killed in a grotesque parody of pregnancy made a coffin.

Another curious device had been placed on a table. Shaped like a pear, made of wood, but with metal attachments and pointed wood pieces set into it. The caption said the torturer put it into a woman's vagina and gradually expanded it inside her body until it broke. Controversy built around this object. Readers wrote letters to the Roman newspaper *Il Messaggero*, complaining that such a thing should be exhibited in public. Finally, someone stole the wooden pear. No one knew, as I remember, how the thief justified his crime, whether the act was motivated by outrage at the insult to the public, that the curators of the exhibit should display such an obscene thing, or whether the theft had been committed by someone aroused, intrigued by the history of the object.

For me, the pear was not the most compelling "machine" on display. There sat, on one of the tables inside the Quirinale Palace, a simple modern device, looking something like a microphone, with electrodes dangling from it. The catalogue acknowledged that critics had objected to the inclusion of this instrument in the exhibit. It was not an antique, lacked the patina of age, the artisanal quality of the other items in the exhibit; even the rack looked hand-fashioned, like something an interior decorator might use to establish atmosphere in a room. But this thing occupied space, calling attention to itself modestly as modern, graceless, banal, ugly.

As I recognized what it must be, pieced together an idea of its functions from recently read accounts of refugees from the Argentinian junta and from Central America, recalled films of the Algerian war, news stories of the reign of the colonels in Greece, this instrument composed of the only too familiar elements of modern technology defamiliarized the devices on exhibit; removing them from the universe of the museum, it identified them with the calculated infliction of human agony. It recontextualized all the other objects, prevented them from being an aesthetic series, snatched them from the realm of the commodified antique, recalled suffering.

The ancient Greeks and Romans routinely tortured slaves as part of their legal systems. So what? Is the recollection of this fact merely a curiosity, a memory of the "antique" which allows us to marvel at our progress from the past of Western culture, our abolition of slavery? Some of us congratulate ourselves on our evolution from a barbaric pagan past, from the world of slave galleys and crucifixions, of *vomitoria* and gladiatorial contests, of pederasty and polytheism. But there is another, supplementary or contestatory narrative told about ancient Greek culture—a narrative about the noble origins of Western civilization. This narrative has analogies with the Quirinale exhibit—it represents the past as a set of detached objects, redolent with antique atmosphere. This alternate and prejudicially selective gaze at the high culture of antiquity, the achievement of those ancient Greeks and Romans to whom we point when we discuss our golden age, produces an ideological text for the whole world now, mythologies about democracy versus communist totalitarianism, about progress, civilized values, human rights. Because we are descended from this noble ancient culture, from the inventors of philosophy and democracy, we see ourselves as privileged, as nobly obliged to guide the whole benighted world toward Western culture's version of democracy and enlightenment. But even as we gaze at high culture, at its origins in antiquity, at its present manifestations in the developed nations, the "base" practices of torturers throughout the world, many of them trained by North Americans, support this narrative by forcing it on others, by making it the hegemonic discourse about history. So-called high culture—philosophical, forensic, civic discourses and practices—is of a piece from the very beginning, from classical antiquity, with the deliberate infliction of human suffering. It is my argument in this book that more is at stake in our recognition of this history than antiquarianism, than complacency about our ad-

4

vances from barbarism to civilization. That truth is unitary, that truth may finally be extracted by torture, is part of our legacy from the Greeks and, therefore, part of our idea of "truth."

Thirty years ago, in an article on torture in Algeria, Jean-Paul Sartre wrote:

> Torture is senseless violence, born in fear. The purpose of it is to force from *one* tongue, amid its screams and its vomiting up of blood, the secret of *everything.* Senseless violence: whether the victim talks or whether he dies under his agony, the secret that he cannot tell is always somewhere else and out of reach. It is the executioner who becomes Sisyphus. If he puts *the question* at all, he will have to continue forever.[1]

Henri Alleg, the victim of torture whose book *La question* occasioned Sartre's essay, recalls one of his torturers boasting that he, the torturer, was the Gestapo, that he was in IndoChina. The Gestapo taught the French, who taught the Americans in Indo-China, and they passed on some of their expertise to the Argentinian, Chilean, El Salvadoran torturers. But this essay is not meant to be a genealogy of modern torture. Rather I am concerned with what Sartre calls "the secret of *everything,*" with the relationship between torture and the truth, which "is always somewhere else and out of reach."

Torture is a terrible and formidable thing. I feel intensely the danger and impertinence of not taking it seriously enough, of speaking about it from the safety of academic America. Though I will write of the etymology of torture and its meaning in ancient Greek culture, I do not want to reduce it to an etymology, or trivialize it as

---

1. Henri Alleg, *The Question*, trans. John Calder, preface by Jean-Paul Sartre (London, 1958), 23.

a literary topos. Rather, I want to show how the logic of our philosophical tradition, of some of our inherited beliefs about truth, leads almost inevitably to conceiving of the body of the other as the site from which truth can be produced, and to using violence if necessary to extract that truth.

I'm concerned here with what surrounds the work of ancient philosophy in particular, the history of the Greek city, relations of gender in antiquity, the kinds of interests philosophy serves even as it claims to have no interests, to be seeking only truth. This essay has several myths of its own origin. One is an essay of Emile Benveniste, "Catégories de pensée et catégories de langue."[2] In this essay Benveniste analyzes how Aristotle's categories, "all the predicates one can affirm of being," are actually categories of the ancient Greek language, dependent on such linguistic features as the middle voice, a self-reflexive voice distinct from the active and passive, the peculiarities of the Greek perfect, et cetera. Aristotle's categories, which exercised and troubled philosophers for centuries, appear to be neither arbitrary nor mirrors of some absolute truth. The linguistic determinism described by Benveniste compels attention; it seems possible to extrapolate from a putative Indo-European social structure, as Benveniste does in other essays, to show how other seeming ideal and abstract concepts are in fact rooted, if not in particular social practices, in the particular historically bound language used to speak about them. Similarly, I want to work out how the Greek philosophical idea of truth was produced in history and what role the social practice of judicial torture played in its production.

I don't want to suggest that the ancient Greeks in-

---

2. Emile Benveniste, *Problèmes de linguistique générale*, vol. 1 (Paris, 1966), 63–74.

vented torture, or that it belongs exclusively to the Western philosophical tradition, or that abhorrence of torture is not also part of that tradition. But I also refuse to adopt the moral stance of those who pretend that torture is the work of "others," that it belongs to the third world, that we can condemn it from afar. To stand thus is to eradicate history, to participate both in the exportation of torture as a product of Western civilization, and in the concealment of its ancient and perhaps necessary coexistence with much that we hold dear. The very idea of truth we receive from the Greeks, those ancestors whom Allan Bloom names for us,[3] is inextricably linked with the practice of torture, which has almost always been the ultimate attempt to discover a secret "always out of reach."

The ancient Greek word for torture is *basanos*. It means first of all the touchstone used to test gold for purity; the Greeks extended its meaning to denote a test or trial to determine whether something or someone is real or genuine. It then comes to mean also inquiry by torture, "the question," torture.[4] In the following pages I will discuss the semantic field of the word *basanos*, its uses in various contexts, both literal and metaphorical. A survey of the place of the *basanos* in the Athenian legal system will follow. This analysis will lead me to consideration of the idea of truth as secret in ancient Greek thought, in literary, ritual, and philosophical practices, and of Plato's characteristically appropriative and idiosyncratic work on the problem of truth. Plato's

---

3. Allan Bloom, *The Closing of the American Mind* (New York, 1988).

4. Liddell and Scott, *Greek English Lexicon*. Hereafter referred to as LSJ.

truth leads to Martin Heidegger's meditations on *alē-theia*, "truth." I will end with some thoughts on the place of truth in the present day, and on the relationship between our inherited ideas about truth and the current widespread use of torture in the world.

# 2 Touchstone

The Greek word *basanos*, in Latin *lapis Lydius*, means "a dark-coloured stone on which pure gold, when rubbed, leaves a peculiar mark" (LSJ).[1] Bankers in antiquity used both scales and touchstones for moneychanging, to assess the value of the many different coins circulating throughout the Aegean world. The *lapis Lydius* was "a flinty slate, black, grey, or white, and the result was judged by the colour of the mark made."[2] In the preclassical period, that is, before the fifth century B.C.E., the word *basanos* appears in the work of aristocratic poets who use it to suggest the necessity for methods of

---

1. Cf. scol. by Chilon ap. Diogenes Laertius 1.71.

2. See T. Hudson-Williams, *The Elegies of Theognis* (New York, 1979 [1910]), 206. See also Pliny, 33.8.

proof of loyalty, in a world in which noble dominance is being threatened, in which the secure place of the descendants of Homeric heroes can no longer be taken for granted. Not only are the poor, citizens or not, challenging the traditional authority of the aristocratic clans in the cities, but even the purity of the aristocrats themselves, supposedly once clearly and unambiguously the good, the *agathoi,* cannot be relied upon absolutely. Many cities in the archaic period immediately preceding the classical age of Greece were rent apart by factionalism among aristocratic clans, struggles for dominance between one great family and another. The stability of the inherited hierarchy was further undermined by the appearance of tyrants, often aristocrats who abandoned their own class to ally with the populace in order to gain hegemony over cities. The occurrence of the metaphor of the touchstone in this period signals an anxiety on the part of those who live in a world turning upside down.[3]

The work of "Theognis"—probably a collective effort produced over time in this period, the sixth century B.C.E., a time of aristocratic factionalism, tyranny, oligarchies, strife between rich and poor—is anxiously concerned with the purity and loyalty of friends; "it is difficult to tell a false friend from a true one."[4] Greed, the desire for gain, leads in the poet's view to betrayal of aristocratic values, of traditional sympotic bonds forged at drinking parties, of fidelity to one's faithful companions. Theognis uses the word *basanos* metaphorically to

---

3. On the changing nature of aristocratic ideology, see Walter Donlan, *The Aristocratic Ideal in Ancient Greece: Attitudes of Superiority from Homer to the End of the Fifth Century B.C.* (Lawrence, Kan., 1980); on the pre-classical crisis, see esp. 77–95.

4. Walter Donlan, "*Pistos Philos Hetairos,*" in *Theognis of Megara: Poetry and the Polis,* ed. Thomas J. Figueira and Gregory Nagy (Baltimore, 1985), 225.

denote a test, a trial to determine whether something is genuine or real,[5] and often employs the word in the context of friendship. For example:

> Seek as I will, I can find no man like myself that is a true comrade [*piston hetairon*] free of guile; and when I am put to the test and tried [*es basanon d'elthôn paratribomenos te*] even as gold is tried beside lead the mark [*tupos*] of pre-eminence is upon me.
>
> (415–18)[6]

The word *paratribomenon*, "rubbed away," alludes directly to the analogy between a test of loyalty and the test of gold by the touchstone.

As Veda Cobb-Stevens has recently pointed out, "The world depicted in the Theognidean corpus is one replete with conflicts, betrayals, duplicities, and uncertainties."[7] The poems of Theognis were produced in a society in crisis, one in which the traditional stable values of the aristocracy have been undermined, in which the wealth and superiority of the good (*agathoi*) have been threatened by the rise of their inferiors (*kakoi*). The poet knows himself to be a "faithful companion," *piston hetairon;* about others he cannot be sure. Later the word *hetairos* comes, in the civil strife of Athens, to denote an aristocratic conspirator, bound in a political club or union,

---

5. Gregory Nagy has recently advanced the theory "that the figure of Theognis represents a cumulative synthesis of Megarian poetic traditions" ("A Poet's Vision of His City," in *Theognis of Megara*, 33.

6. *Elegy and Iambus*, ed. and trans. J.M. Edmonds (Cambridge, Mass., 1932).

7. Veda Cobb-Stevens, "Opposites, Reversals, and Ambiguities: The Unsettled World of Theognis," in *Theognis of Megara*, 159.

and often opposed to the democracy. In sixth-century Megara, the "companions" are discerned only with difficulty; inferiors have used deceit to effect their overthrow of the order (*kosmos*) of the past; Theognis uses ambiguous, riddling language to preserve his message for those worthy to receive it.[8]

The text of Theognis boasts of the purity of the poet himself in language evoking the purity of metals. It claims that he alone stands faithful to the old order now lost:

> If you would wash me, the water will flow unsullied [*amianton*] from my head; you will find me in all matters as it were refined gold, red to the view when I be rubbed with the touchstone [*eruthron idein tribomenon basanôi*]; the surface of me is untainted of black mould or rust, its bloom ever pure and clean [*katharon*].
>
> (447–52)[9]

The poet resembles the purest gold, untouched by any pollution or *miasma*, clean, like a ritual instrument or a sacrificial victim. Gold, that material least liable to corruption, is for him an emblem of extraordinary integrity and stability in human character.

The desire for a reliable test to determine the fidelity of a suspect intimate recurs in Greek poetry, and later poets often employ the metaphor of the testing of metal to describe the necessity and unreliability of testing for the fidelity of friends. The Lydians of Asia Minor had invented the use of metal currency, of money, in the

---

8. Cf. scol. by Chilon ap. Diogenes Laertius 1.71.

9. Cf. Bacchylides fr. 10, in which he mentions the *basanos: Ludia men gar lithos manuei khruson,* "for the Lydian stone reveals gold." The verb *manuô,* in Attic *menuô,* was used in Athens of informers, who "reveal, inform, or betray."

seventh century B.C.E. The *polis* or city-state of Aegina was reputed to be the first Greek city to establish a silver coinage; in the classical period several different coinages circulated. By the fifth century B.C.E. coins of small enough denominations existed to enter into the economic transactions of daily life. In Euripides' *Hippolytus* the Athenian king Theseus, bewildered by contradictory accounts of an alleged seduction attempt by his son against his wife, uses monetary language to convey his confusion about the mysteries of domestic intimacy:

> Theseus: If there were some token now, some mark to make the division clear between friend and friend, the true and the false!
>
> (924–26)

Theseus employs the language of the banker, of the money-lender, to suggest that one of his friends, that is, of those dear to him, either his son or his wife, is false and counterfeit.

Theognis, a century before, uses the word *amianton*, unpolluted, to describe the water which might be thought necessary to cleanse him. *Miainô*, in the verbal form, means to paint over, stain, dye, color, and thus to stain, defile, soil. In the text of Theognis, the word *amianton*, a negative adjective formed from *miainô* and the so-called alpha privative, belongs to a powerful complex of terms; pollution is a religious term, connected with the impurity of blood shed, of unclean sacrificial practices or murder.[10] In the archaic period, the state of freedom from pollution is sometimes connected with notions of inherited purity, of uncontaminated descent from the generations of heroes, from the gods, ideas of

---

10. See Robert Parker, *Miasma: Pollution and Purification in Early Greek Religion* (Oxford, 1983).

inherited excellence through which the aristocrats justified their dominance in the archaic cities.

The *basanos*, an imaginary tool for the testing of
friendship, loyalty, and adherence to traditional values,
provides a central metaphor for Theognis's verse. The
poet himself passes the test of the touchstone; others,
who have betrayed him and the world he sees fast slipping away, would be exposed as base metal by the ordeal.

Another aristocratic poet, Pindar, also conceives of the
*basanos* metaphorically as an instrument for separating
the good from the base.[11] In *Pythian* 10, the poet ends his
song, a complex hymn of praise to a victor in a footrace,
with praise of the boy's father, Thorax of Larissa.[12] The
poem echoes with the Pindaric themes of the brevity of
contact with the divine, the chasm between mortal and
immortal; it evokes the myth of the Hyperboreans, a
mythic people who lived beyond the north wind, who
were visited by Perseus, ancestor of Thorax. Pindar
praises Thorax for having commissioned his song, and
adds:

Gold and a straight mind show what they are on the
touchstone [*en basanôi*]. (67)[13]

---

11. See also Bacchylides, fr. 10: *Ludia men gar lithos manuei
khruson, andrôn d'aretan sophia te pagkrates t'elegkhei alatheia:*
"for the Lydian stone reveals gold, but all-powerful wisdom
and truth cross-examine the excellence of men."

12. On this poem, and on the Pindaric tradition, see William Fitzgerald, *Agonistic Poetry. The Pindaric Mode in Pindar,
Horace, Hölderlin, and the English Ode* (Berkeley, 1987), esp.
p. 54.

13. *Pindar's Victory Songs*, trans. Frank J. Nisetich (Baltimore and London, 1980), 218.

The upright mind (*noos orthos*), like the refined, golden surface of the Theognidean poet, like the true comrade, survives the test of the *basanos* and is shown to be purely itself, uncontaminated, unalloyed. In Pindar's text, the word *basanos*, which follows a set of allusions to the ancestry of the poet's patron, to the victories of son, father, grandfather, distant heroic and divine antecedents, suggests the verification of the unalloyed purity of aristocratic blood. The very last lines of the poem echo the concerns of Theognis, a recognition of the political disturbances of the ancient city, and the desire of the aristocratic poet for a steady hand, sanctioned by blood and tradition, at the city's helm:

> Let us praise
> his brave brothers too, because
> they bear on high the ways of Thessaly
> and bring them glory.
>> In their hands
> belongs the piloting of cities, their fathers'
>> heritage.
>
> (68–72)

This last phrase might be rendered: "in the care of the good men [Theognis's *agathoi*, a political term] lie the inherited, paternal pilotings, governings [following the metaphor of the ship of state] of cities." The city is a ship that must be guided by those who are capable by birth of piloting it, that is to say, the *agathoi*, the good, the aristocrats. The *basanos* reveals the good, separates base metal from pure gold, aristocrat from commoner.

Pindar metaphorically subjects his own work, his own song, to the *basanos* in *Nemean* 8, another poem in honor of a victor in a footrace, another son whose father had won an earlier victory. Like the *agathoi* of *Pythian* 10, whose nobility of birth and conduct meets the test of the touchstone, the poet's words will encounter an ordeal:

*15*

I stand on light feet now,
   catching breath before I speak
For there are songs in every style,
but to put a new one to the touchstone [*basanôi*]
for testing [*es elegkhon*] is all danger.
                            Words are a morsel
     to the envious,
and their envy always
fastens on the noble,
                     but leaves the base alone.
                           (19–22)

The poem circles around the theme of envy, the envy of the losers in an athletic contest for the victor, of Pindar's fellow poets for his superior skill, the envy of the hero Aias for Odysseus' victory in a contest for the arms of Achilles.

Pindar addresses the issue of democracy in his cryptic way here. The victor for whom the poem is composed is an Aeginetan, from the island of Aegina near Athens which in Pindar's day represented the ideological contrary of the democratic city. Athens in the late sixth and early fifth centuries constructed a new form of government, *dêmokratia*, people's rule; Aegina was ruled by an oligarchy, a small group of ancient and noble families who based their hereditary claims to domination of the city on blood-lines traced back to the heroes of the Trojan War and beyond, to the gods. Pindar celebrates the legendary Aeginetan king Aiakos, son of Zeus and Aegina, renowned for his exercise of justice. The poet then moves to the tale of the death of Aias, descendant of Aiakos, linking it with characteristic indirection to his theme of base men's envy for the noble. In the vote concerning who would inherit the arms of the great hero Achilles, killed before Troy, envy destroyed Aias. And in an oblique reference perhaps to the newly invented practices of democracy, Pindar alters the traditional version of the legend and says those judging the contest for the armor between Aias (Ajax) and Odysseus used "secret ballots," *kruphiaisi psaphoi* (26). In the traditional Homeric or Hesiodic mode of judgment, a wise king or a group of noble elders rendered their verdict openly, in a public assembly. Wounded by what he saw as his comrades' betrayal, in Pindar's version a betrayal made possible by corrupt and democratically tainted secrecy, Aias committed suicide, envious of Odysseus's prize; Pindar suggests that envy of Aias's greatness, a leveling impulse, perhaps, led the Danaans to vote against the greater hero: "they gave the best prize to the glistening lie" (25).

The language of the poem evokes the traditional contrast drawn between Aias, hero of battle, man of few words, and Odysseus, the plotter, the rhetorician before his time. Pindar alludes darkly to the present as a time similarly balanced between ancient heroic values and slippery tongues: "Yes, hateful slander [*ekhthra parphasis*] existed also [*kai*] long ago" (translation modified). Pindar makes an implicit analogy between his own song and the courage and nobility of Aias; he too will suffer envious words and the deluded judgment of the people. "For there are songs in every style, / but to put a new one to the touchstone [*basanôi*] for testing is all danger" (20–21). The metaphor of the *basanos* here signifies the problematic of judgment, test, ordeal, but the fragile Theognidean confidence that the truth will out has disappeared. Envy will attack the noble (22), *eslon*, a word which like *agathoi* denotes goodness and connotes wealth, nobility, inherited power. Envy does not strive with base men, called *kheironessi*, the comparative form of Theognis's *kakoi*, no longer the bad, but the worse. This too is a politically charged term; *hoi kheirones* are "men of lower degree" (LSJ). The world has changed; the *basanos*, no longer the sure test of purity for which Theognis hoped, has itself been corrupted, become an occasion for envy. Pindar tells the double story of his

17

own poetic practice, his offering to his patron, and of the
ordeal of Aias. In his retrospective gaze, envy attacks
and has always attacked the best man: "envy always /
fastens on the noble" (21–22). In his present, the poet's
audience constitutes the *basanos*, the touchstone. And
the public arena has become a contested sphere in which
the secure oligarchic dominance of an aristocracy and
its poets cannot be assumed, in which the secret ballots
of the people, the judgment of a base audience, can
award the prize of political power, of artistic preemi-
nence, to another. The democratic processes of the lot
and the secret ballot threaten to eliminate the traditional justice based on the innate superiority and judgment of a few noble men.


The tragic poet Sophokles alludes to the touchstone in
his plays concerning Oedipus, playing with the word's
ambiguous reference to the literal touchstone, to some
sort of ordeal demonstrating men's fidelity, to the place
the word has in Athenian legal parlance. In *Oedipus Rex*,
the chorus recalls the history of the *tyrannos*, the tyrant-
king of Thebes. They have just witnessed the terrible
scene between Teiresias and Oedipus, in which the tyrant hears the truth of his crimes, but does not understand. Teiresias has said:

> You have your eyes but see not where you are in sin,
> nor where you live, nor whom you live with.
> (413–14)

Oedipus will lose his eyes when he does at last see where
he is, where he lives, with whom he lives. The chorus
at this moment in the tragedy cannot choose between
Teiresias and Oedipus, cannot judge. Twice they use the
word *basanos* to denote a wished-for instrument of proof,

some sign from elsewhere that would relieve them from
the burden of choice:

> I never heard in the present
> nor past of a quarrel between
> the sons of Labdacus and Polybus,
> that I might bring as proof [*basanôi*]
> in attacking the popular fame
> of Oedipus. . . .
>
> (489–94)

> Truly Zeus and Apollo are wise
> and in human things all knowing;
> but amongst men there is no
> distinct judgment [*krisis alēthês*], between
>   the prophet
> and me—which of us is right.
> One man may pass another in wisdom
> but I would never agree
> with those that find fault with the king
> till I should see the word
> proved right beyond doubt. For once
> in visible form the Sphinx
> came on him and all of us
> saw his wisdom and in that test [*basanôi*]
> he saved the city.
>
> (498–510)

The chorus is caught between the seer Teiresias and the
king Oedipus, between the conflicting values of religious
vision and benevolent tyranny. In their confusion, they
seek a touchstone, some proof establishing which of
these two discourses is true. They recall Oedipus' former
subjection to a touchstone, the ordeal of the Sphinx's
riddle, and his successful passage of that test. His intelli-

gence and audacity are posed against the divine authority of the prophet.

The legal language of this choral ode suggests the social context of Greek tragedy; the tragic performances of the classical city have many affinities with the law courts of Athens. The chorus has the collective character of a jury. Like the athletic contests celebrated by Pindar, both legal debates and the confrontations of characters in tragedy are *agones*, "gatherings," and struggles, contests.[14] Jean-Pierre Vernant has illuminated our understanding of the place of tragedy in the ancient city by pointing out the ways in which the legal and the tragic are intertwined.

> The tragic writers' use of a technical legal vocabulary underlines the affinities between the most favoured tragic themes and certain cases which fell within the competence of the courts. The institution of these courts was sufficiently recent for the novelty of the values determining their establishment and governing their activity still to be fully appreciated. The tragic poets make use of this legal vocabulary, deliberately exploiting its ambiguities, its fluctuations and its incompleteness. We find an imprecision in the terms used, shifts of meaning, incoherences and contradictions all of which reveal the disagreements within legal thought itself.[15]

The words of the chorus in the Oedipus ode have the status Vernant describes, one of imprecision, ambiguity,

---

14. On tragedy and law, see Richard Garner, *Law and Society in Classical Athens* (London, 1987).

15. Jean-Pierre Vernant, "The Historical Moment of Tragedy in Greece," *Tragedy and Myth in Ancient Greece*, ed. J.-P. Vernant and Pierre Vidal-Naquet, trans. Janet Lloyd (Atlantic Highlands, New Jersey, 1981), 3.

fluctuation. The oracle at Delphi has accused Thebes of harboring a murderer, a killer who must be found out, who in a legal trial would be accused, tried, judged, punished. The legal language of judgment echoes throughout the ode. The members of the chorus have no *basanos* with which to test the possibility of enmity between Labdakos's sons and Polybos, no *krisis alêthês*, true judgment, by which they might choose between the words of Teiresias and their loyalty to Oedipus. Oedipus, in his contest with the winged maiden, the Sphinx, another test, *basanos*, was seen as wise and dear to the people, *hadupolis*, but now Thebes' citizens are lost in world without clear signs. The language of the tragedy fluctuates between the lyric use of *basanos* as a metaphor, a concrete allusion to the touchstone which exposes the impurity of alloyed metal, and a more assimilated use, in which the metaphor is somewhat obscured.

The Sophoclean language, and its ambiguity, reveal the gradual transition of the meaning of the word *basanos* from "test" to "torture." The literal meaning, "touchstone," gives way to a figurative meaning, "test," then over time changes to "torture," as the analogy is extended to the testing of human bodies in juridical procedures for the Athenian courts. Is the history of *basanos* itself in ancient Athens a process of refiguration, the alienation of the test from a metal to the slave, the other? Such a transfer is literally catachresis, the improper use of words, the application of a term to a thing which it does not properly denote, abuse or perversion of a trope or metaphor (*OED*); George Puttenham, the Elizabethan rhetorician, calls catachresis "the figure of abuse." The modern English word touchstone is similarly employed by people who have no idea of the archaic reference to the *lapis Lydius*, also called in English basanite. The figurative use of the word *touchstone* has taken the place of the literal meaning.

In Greek, the lines from *Oedipus Rex* seems to mark a transitional moment in the use of the word *basanos;* the legal atmosphere of a homicide accusation colors the tragedy, along with the notion, also connotative of the legal, of *krisis*, judgment. But the chorus can also evoke the denotative use of the term *basanos*, one familiar from the lyric poets Theognis and Pindar. Is King Oedipus worthy of his station? Is he truly *hadupolis*, sweet, dear to the people? Or is he a counterfeit king? Oedipus is an intermediate figure, between the unfaithful comrade, *hetairos*—condemned by both Theognis and the *basanos* as unworthy of aristocratic affection and popular support—and a prisoner in the dock, ready for the judgment, the *krisis* of a jury which may use another kind of *basanos*, the ordeal by torture, to discover the truth. In the lines which follow those cited above, Kreon uses the language of the courtroom to address the chorus:

> Citizens, I have come because I heard
> deadly words spread about me, that the king
> accuses [*katêgorein*] me.
>
> (512–15)

The vocabulary of the scene includes *zêmia*, "penalty," "fine" (520), *katêgoreito*, "accuse" (529); Kreon says: "Will you listen to words to answer yours, and then pass judgment [*krin'*]?" (543–44). The question parodies the situation in the law court; Oedipus as tyrant is both antagonist and judge. In the next scene Oedipus accuses Kreon:

> And you are wrong if you believe that one,
> a criminal, will not be punished [*huphexein tên dikên*] only
> because he is my kinsman.
>
> (551–53)

*Dikê* means justice; it also means a trial, a lawsuit; Kreon would, as a criminal, be required to "give an account" of his crime, but also to submit to a lawsuit. Oedipus himself will be forced to undergo a further testing, another *basanos;* guilty but unpunished, he will blind himself.

The forensic language of *Oedipus Rex* fuses heroic legend with the poetic representation of the city's institutions. The mythic narrative of Oedipus's encounter with the Sphinx, set in the most remote past, and the struggle between Kreon and Oedipus over the investigation of an ancient and mythic homicide, here meet the daily life of the democratic *polis*. The language of Sophokles' tragedy might be said to exemplify not only the contradictions between the tyranny of the fictional past and the "secret ballots," alluded to disparagingly by Pindar, of the audience's present, but also to represent dramatically, in an almost utopian manner, a synthesis of the Greeks' legendary origins and their political processes. The chorus's attempt to judge Oedipus resembles the aristocratic reveler's testing of his fellow symposiasts, using as it does archaic, lyric language; it is also like the democratic jury's testing of a citizen on trial, alluding obliquely at the same time to the juridical torture of slaves in the Athenian legal system, a process which by this time was referred to as the *basanos.*

Some of the semantic processes that transformed *basanos* as touchstone into the term for legal torture can be seen in the use of the term in the *Oedipus Coloneus*. This tragedy is only obliquely concerned with the process of democracy, with the new institutions of the mid-fifth century which mediated between the city's aristocratic past and its democratic present. It speaks instead of the exhaustion of the political, of disillusionment with parties and with war, of metaphysical solutions to problems too bitter to be resolved in mortal *agones*. In a brutal scene between Kreon, now tyrant of Thebes, and the aged, blind Oedipus, Kreon attempts to carry Oedipus off to Thebes,

to deny Athens his blessing. Failing to convince Oedipus
to return to Thebes, he tries to abduct Oedipus's daughter
and companion, Antigone, while the chorus protests:

What are you doing, stranger? Will you
Let her go? Must we have a test of strength? [*takh'es*
  *basanon ei kherôn*]

(834–35)

Sophokles attenuates the metaphor of the touchstone,
removing it from the quotidian realm of moneychanging
even more in this passage than in *Oedipus Rex*. Here it
is not even clear who is being tested; rather, the word
*basanos* suggests violence, the contest of hands. Literally, the text says, "Soon you will come to a *basanos*
of hands." Hand strikes against hand. The *basanos*, no
longer an autonomous, inert, inanimate tool for assaying
metal, has become a struggle between two forces, a contest that assumes physical violence, a reconcretizing of
the "touchstone," which is neither the literal stone nor a
metaphorical ordeal. Hands, pitted one against the
other, rematerialize the test. The touchstone sets stone
against metal; the test of friends sets one against another; here the *agôn*, the contest implicit in the notion
of *basanos*, takes on a new connotation, one of combat
between enemies.

Some historians of the ancient city believe that the
word *basanos* refers not to physical torture, but to a
legal interrogation that does not involve violence. Others
claim that the threat of torture may have been present
in the word, but that there is no evidence that torture
was actually ever practiced.[16] It seems to me very un-

---

16. On torture, see R. Turasiewicz, *De servis testibus in
Atheniensium iudiciis* (Cracow, 1963).

likely, even though the ancient evidence does not describe directly any single case of torture, that the frequent mentions of *basanos* in contexts of physical intimidation can refer to anything but the practice of torture. The accidents of survival of ancient material may mean that we have no single documented instance of torture having been applied, but the many uses of the term, not only in the context of the law court, suggest a cultural acceptance of the meaning "torture" for *basanos*, and an assumption that torture occurred. For example, the historian Herodotos, in recounting an incident that took place during the Persian Wars, in the early years of the fifth century B.C.E., describes the Athenian hero Themistokles' secret negotiations with the Persian emperor Xerxes after the battle of Salamis:

> Themistocles lost no time in getting a message through to Xerxes. The men he chose for this purpose were all people he could trust to keep his instructions secret [*sigan*], even under torture [*es pasan basanon*].
>
> 8.110

This passage suggests not only that *basanos* was not merely interrogation, but that with the meaning torture it formed part of the vocabulary of daily life, and that torture figured in the relations between ancient states as well as in the legal processes of the democratic city. Themistokles had to take into account the ability of his emissaries to resist physical torture, *pasan basanon*, "any, all torture," when deciding whom to send to the Persian emperor. He required silence under extreme interrogation, since he was claiming falsely to have protected Xerxes from the pursuit of the Greeks after the Persians' defeat. And Herodotos uses the word *basanos* as if the meaning "torture" were common currency.

As do Sophokles' Oedipus plays, Herodotos's text offers a double vision, providing further evidence about the place of torture in the democracy and in its prehistory. Sophokles writes from within the democracy about episodes from the archaic, legendary past of the city. Herodotos writes from the world of the mid-fifth century, the time of Sophokles and the great imperial age of Athens, looking back half a century. The victories of Athens in the Persian Wars had enabled and produced the great flowering of Athenian culture and ambition in the middle of the fifth century. Herodotos's retrospective gaze at the origins of the democracy and its empire paints the portrait of Themistokles, one of the great aristocrats whose power and vision shaped the evolution of the democratic city. His encouragement, for example, of the policy of spending the city's mining wealth on its fleet, rather than distributing of monies to the citizens, meant that the poorest citizens in Athens, who manned the fleet, participated actively and powerfully in the political and military decisions of the following years. In the incident Herodotos describes, Themistokles takes care to ensure that his self-interested machinations not be known by the Athenians he led. Themistokles, like Oedipus, has become a creature of legend.

The possible use of the *basanos* by the Persians may suggest the Greeks' impression of its barbaric nature; the "other" is often said to be the inventor and abuser of torture. Herodotos may also be projecting from the Athenian legal institutions of the latter part of the century onto this episode, which led directly to the deception of the Persian emperor and to the triumph of the Athenians over the retreating emperor.

Silence under torture may be coded as an aristocratic virtue. A notorious aspect of the training of the elite Spartan youth involved the inculcation of stamina and endurance in trying circumstances. Although our evidence for the practices of the Spartans in this regard is often late, we do hear of the incident of the Spartan boy caught with a fox trapped in his clothing, who remains silent as the fox gnaws at his vitals. Although the story may be apocryphal, part of the elaborate set of narrative *topoi* used by the Athenians to differentiate themselves from the Lakedaimonians, often by authors of aristocratic sympathy who accuse democratic Athens of softness—nonetheless, it indicates the degree to which silence under pain is ideologically associated with nobility. The slave has no resources through which to resist submitting to pain and telling all. In contrast the aristocratic soldier, noble by both birth and training, maintains laconic silence in the face of physical abuse.

A similar reference to torture in war occurs in the later text of Thucydides. In this case, the Athenian generals Nikias and Demosthenes were put to death by the Syracusans after the Athenians' defeat in Sicily. Arguing against the position that Demosthenes should be spared so that he could be brought in triumph to the Athenians' enemies the Spartans, the Syracusans decided that if Nikias were spared he might betray some of their intrigues under torture (*basanizomenos;* 7.86). Thucydides cannot declare absolutely that this was the Syracusans' reasoning, in his scrupulous practice of recording the past, but it was "for this reason or for a reason very near to this" that Nikias, a man whom he greatly admired, was put to death.


In literary texts the poets treat the notion of *basanos* for the most part metaphorically, as Sophokles does, as a test, without the catachrestic use of "touchstone" for torture. Although the term *basanos* is not used in the *Oresteia*, in the last play of the trilogy, the *Eumenides*, Aeschylus nonetheless refers to physical punishment. The god Apollo, in a horrified and misogynist rant, seeks to chase the Furies from his sanctuary at Delphi. He expresses his disgust at their appearance, and at their associations with primitive forms of justice, in this address:

> This house is no right place for such as you to
>   cling
> upon; but where, by judgment given, heads are
>   lopped
> and eyes gouged out, throats cut, and by the spoil
>   of sex
> the glory of young boys is defeated, where
>   mutilation
> lives, and stoning, and the long moan of tortured
>   men
> spiked underneath the spine and stuck on pales.
>                         (*Eumenides* 185–90)[17]

These lines may not refer to contemporary Delphic or Athenian practices of execution or mutilation.[18] Apollo here attributes these atrocities to the imaginary reign of the Furies, an archaic, bloody domain of cruelty and vengeance. Throughout the *Oresteia*, such practices are associated with a past that must be transcended, in Athens, in this final play of the trilogy, through the establishment of the Areopagus, a court that judges cases of homicide by means of law, without regression to the endless

---

17. *Aeschylus, vol. I: Oresteia,* trans. Richmond Lattimore, ed. David Grene and Richmond Lattimore (Chicago, 1953).

18. See Louis Gernet, "Some Connections between Punishment and Religion in Ancient Greece" and "Capital Punishment," in *The Anthropology of Ancient Greece,* trans. John Hamilton and Blaise Nagy (Baltimore, 1981), 240–76, and *Du chatiment dans la cité. Supplices corporels et peine de mort dans le monde antique* (Rome, 1984), esp. Eva Cantarella, "Per una preistoria del castigo," 37–73, on the *apotumpanismos,* the binding of a condemned criminal to a stake as a form of execution.

cycle of revenge Aeschylus represents as characteristic of the old days. Apollo, the beautiful young male god of philosophy, music and prophecy, locates the Furies in a space and time characterized not only by beheading, throat cutting, stoning, and impalement, but also, most prominently, by castration. Aeschylus and his god represent women as the most bloodthirsty and violent of human beings, displacing the cruelty of the state onto these archaic figures of vengeance.[19]

These references to mutilation and execution are unusual in the corpus of Greek tragedy. But if there is something like a denial of the application of the term *basanos* to the literal ordeal of the body in torture in the realm of tragedy, Aristophanes refers to the *basanos* explicitly in his comedies, in a manner that anticipates the direct and matter-of-fact discussion of *basanos* as torture in many legal texts. Unlike tragedy, comedy refers to quotidian experience, mocking it, estranging it, holding it up to the ridicule of the crowd, sometimes domesticating the most unpalatable aspects of ancient life.

We find a comic parody of the use of *basanos* for the courtroom in Aristophanes' *Frogs*.[20] The comedy is devoted to themes of judgment, discrimination, and eval-

---

19. See Froma Zeitlin, "The Dynamics of Misogyny: Myth and Mythmaking in the *Oresteia*," in *Women in the Ancient World: The Arethusa Papers*, ed. J. Peradotto and J. P. Sullivan (Albany, 1984), 149–84, and Marcel Detienne, "Violentes *eugénies*," in *La cuisine du sacrifice*, ed. Detienne and Jean-Pierre Vernant (Paris, 1979).

20. For a brilliant reading of this play, see David Konstan, "Poésie, politique et rituel dans les *Grenouilles* d'Aristophane," *Métis* 1 (1986), 291–308. Konstan describes a trajectory in the ancient city from a stage of the individual transcendence of the hero, through a phase of ritual solidarity, to an agonistic and dialogical contest that mediates these two preceding forms (307).

uation. Dionysos and his slave Xanthias have set off
on a journey to Hades to retrieve the tragic poet
Euripides, but end by choosing Aeschylus to bring back
with them, claiming him over Euripides as the superior
poet. Dionysos had dressed for the trip as Herakles, who
had once successfully entered and, more importantly,
departed the realm of the dead, but when he learns
that Herakles is *persona non grata* in Hades, he forces
his slave to trade costumes with him. When Xanthias
is mistaken for Herakles and about to be arrested as
a dog-napper, for the stealing of Kerberos, the slave
offers to give up his own supposed slave, really the
god Dionysos, to torture:

> You give this slave of mine the third degree
> [*basanize*]
>
> > > (616)

The judge asks, "And how may I torture him?" (*pôs ba-
sanisô;* 618), and the real slave Xanthias, not real at all
but an actor playing a slave playing at being the god
Dionysos, says:

> Why anything!
> The rack, the wheel, the whip . . . Skin him alive
>   . . .
> Vinegar up his nose . . . bricks on his chest . . .
> Or hang him by his thumbs . . . what have you
>   . . . *But*
> No lashing with a leek or onion top!
>
> > > (618–22)

The catalogue of torture devices here is most instructive.
We find binding to the ladder (*klimaki;* later a rhetorical
term); the whip (*hustrikhis*) routinely used for punishing
slaves, the name of which is derived from the word for
hedgehog or porcupine, and which suggests sharp

spines; flaying; stretching on the rack (*streblôn*). Further techniques involve drowning him in vinegar, that is, sour wine, the further fermentation of the liquid of Dionysos, piling bricks on him; proscribed are the ritual beatings administered with leeks that are characteristic of *pharmakos* or scapegoat rituals like the Thargelia.[21]

Aiakos, the judge of Hades, promises to reimburse Xanthias if the torture maims his slave, but Xanthias refuses the offer and urges him to lead the slave off for torture. When Dionysos claims to be a god, Xanthias retorts:

> All the more reason, then, to torture him . . .
> [*mastigôteos*] . . .
> Won't even feel it, if he is a god!
>
> (633–34)

The result is a beating contest in which Xanthias seems sure to win, accustomed as he, a real slave, is to such beatings. The beatings constitute not punishment but torture, and the language of the comedy reflects this fact. The torture will reveal the truth, show which of the two is a god, which a slave. The comedy works on the reversal of slave and god; Xanthias claims a god would not be hurt by a beating, but the slave, the lowest of mortal beings, might in fact be thought, because of experience, most easily to endure a whipping. Dionysos begins to weep under the beating, but claims it's due to onions. Aiakos is finally unable to decide which of the two is divine.

In the parabasis, the address to the audience, that follows, the theme of noble and base currency emerges once again, as if connected by free association with this

---

21. Walter Burkert, *Greek Religion*, trans. John Raffan (Cambridge, Mass., 1985), 82–84.

scene of torture, of the *basanos* or touchstone. The chorus
appeals to the Athenian populace, complaining that
Athenians who had committed one fault in a battle at
sea were to be put to death, while slaves who had fought
alongside their masters had been given their freedom.
This seems to the chorus to be a perversion of traditional
hierarchical thinking:

> It appears to us that Athens shows the selfsame
>   attitude
> To the fairest and the purest and the noblest
>   [*kalous te kagathous*] of her brood,
> As toward our silver coinage and the later
>   wartime gold,
> Both of which are out of fashion, though their
>   worth has been extolled
> As the finest ever minted. All men everywhere
>   agree
> That their weight and sterling soundness are
>   unique in currency,
> Whether here at home in Hellas or abroad. But
>   recently
> We ourselves no longer like them, and prefer to
>   use for cash
> A debased barbaric tender—this new-fangled
>   copper trash!
> So, too, *men* of weight and substance, Hellenes to
>   the manner born,
> Men of rounded education and of sterling worth,
>   we scorn.
>
> (718–730)

The Athenians now honor base men, as they mint base
coins. The metaphor of metals recalls Theognis's poems
of testing with the touchstone. Aristophanes returns to
this archaic formulation of the relative worth of men,
using language familiar since Hesiod's myth of the ages

of men, compared to metals. The scene of mock torture prepares for this plea for a return to true value. Men of state must be put to the test, slaves and foreigners must no longer be rewarded as if they were valuable, superior, golden.

The scene of mock torture, of the beating of Dionysos and his slave, not only sets up the chorus's appeal to the audience's sense of traditional hierarchy; it also shows how commonplace is the language of testing and torture in the ancient city. The comic beating is quite hilarious, of course. But it does not put into question the reality of torture. The exchange has a carnival quality, Dionysos masquerading as slave, slave masquerading as Dionysos masquerading as Herakles, the god beaten like a common slave. The slave remains uppity and insolent, the god cowardly and ridiculous. Comedy permits this representation of the quotidian reality of the *polis*, the exposure of what cannot be alluded to directly in tragedy, the violence and domination implicit in the situation of bondage. Comedy allows the fictional depiction of the unspeakable, the representation of the lowly slave, the allusion to ordinary cruelty, a commentary on the difficulty of perceiving the essential difference between divine and enslaved beings.

But the referent of all of this is torture, and the humor depends on the audience's sense of the incongruity of the god tortured, not on the incongruity or cruelty of beating and whipping and torture *per se*. In classical culture citizens take slavery for granted, and physical punishment and torture are part of the institution of slavery. Seneca tells of a man who planned to execute a slave who had broken a crystal cup by having him thrown as food to lampreys (*Dialogue* 5: *On Anger* 3:40). If Aristophanes is so iconoclastic as to mock the gods, and to treat the slave as if he were a human character, he does not

go so far as to question the institution of the *basanos.*
More explicitly than in the Sophoclean example from
*Oedipus Rex,* this scene evokes the courtroom. Aiakos is
judge, Xanthias master, Dionysos the slave whose evidence will be obtained under torture.

# 3          The Law

The Greeks first use the literal meaning for *basanos* of "touchstone," then metaphorize it to connote a test, then reconcretize, rematerialize it to mean once again a physical testing in torture. If a coin or bit of metal, applied to the touchstone, marks the stone in a distinctive way, how is this process figured in relation to the human body? The slave on the rack waits like the metal, pure or alloyed, to be tested. The test, the touchstone, is the process of torture—the ladder, the whip, the rack, all those techniques catalogued by Aristophanes. But the test is not identical to that described by Theognis, in which the good man figuratively interrogates another, questioning his loyalty. Rather, this test assumes that the slave, because of his or her servile status, will not spontaneously produce a pure statement, cannot be trusted to do so. The test assumes that its result will be truth; the truth concerning a tested metal, whether or not it is the sought-after "gold," is the alienated product of the earlier test. The truth is generated by torture from the speech of the slave; the sounds of the slave on the rack must by definition contain truth, which the torture produces. And when set against other testimony in a court case, that necessary truth, like a touchstone itself, will show up the truth or falsity of the testimony. The process of testing has been spun out from the simple metallurgist's experiment, to a new figuration of the work of interrogating matter. It is the slave's body, not metal, which receives the test; but how can that body be demonstrated to be true or false, pure or alloyed, loyal or disloyal? The *basanos* assumes first that the slave always lies, then that torture makes him or her always tell the truth, then that the truth produced through torture will always expose the truth or falsehood of the free man's evidence.

The Athenians, notorious for their litigiousness, mention the *basanos* frequently in speeches we believe were written for the court. I want to look now at the ways in which forensic orators speak of the *basanos*. Although they sometimes use the term to denote a careful scrutiny of evidence or the like, the "touchstone" in their texts usually is no longer a stone, no longer a metaphor for a test; *basanos* has become the word in common Athenian usage for what litigants do to slaves when they become implicated in a court case.[1]

*Basanos* as an element of the Athenian legal system is somewhat neglected by those who praise that system

---

1. On the question of whether free noncitizens could be tortured in homicide cases and cases of wounding with intent to kill, see C. Carey, "A Note on Torture in Athenian Homicide Cases," *Historia* 37:8 (1988), 241–45. Carey summarizes the evidence and concludes that torture was probably limited to slaves in both types of cases.

as one of the Athenians' greatest achievements. D. M. MacDowell, for example, author of a definitive book on Greek law, says:

> The Athenians' legal system, though less coherent than the Romans' a few centuries later, was probably the most comprehensive that any people had yet devised, and was certainly the first to be established on a democratic basis.[2]

Yet the Athenian democracy was at best a sort of oligarchy, one that denied legal and political rights to all women, even daughters of citizens, and to foreigners and slaves residing in Attica. The practice of slave torture is consistent with the democracy's policies of exclusion, scapegoating, ostracism, and physical cruelty and violence; to overlook or justify torture is to misrecognize and idealize the Athenian state.

MacDowell describes the place of torture in the Athenian legal system:

> A special rule governed the testimony of slaves: they could not appear in court, but a statement which a slave, male or female, had made under torture (*basanos*) could be produced in court as evidence.[3]

The party in a trial who wished a slave to be tortured would put his questions in writing, specifying which slaves he wished to have tortured and the questions they were to be asked, and also agreeing to pay the slave's owner for any permanent damage inflicted on the slave. Athenian citizens could not be tortured.

---

2. D. M. MacDowell, *The Law in Classical Athens* (London, 1978), 8.

3. *Ibid.*, 245.

MacDowell reasons as follows about the rule that slave's testimony could be received in the courtroom *only* if the slave had been tortured:

> The reason for this rule must have been that a slave who knew anything material would frequently belong to one of the litigants, and so would be afraid to say anything contrary to his owner's interests, unless the pressure put on him to reveal the truth was even greater than the punishment for revealing it which he could expect from his master.[4]

A. R. W. Harrison believes that the right to testify freely in court may have been seen as a privilege, perhaps because witnesses who appeared in court were once thought of as "compurgators," witnesses who swore to the credibility of a party in a law suit. "Torture must therefore be applied to the slave as a mark of the fact that he was not in himself a free agent entitled to support one side or the other."[5] Since the slave was a valuable piece of property, liable to damage from torture, she or he could not be tortured without permission of the owner.[6] If that permission were denied, the opponent often claimed that the evidence which would have been obtained under torture would of certainty have been damning to the slave's owner.

---

4. *Ibid.*

5. A. R. W. Harrison, *The Law of Athens*, vol. 2, *Procedure* (Oxford, 1971), 147.

6. See also R. J. Bonner and Gertrude Smith, *The Administration of Justice from Homer to Aristotle*, vol. 2 (Chicago, 1938), 221–29, J. Walter Jones, *The Law and Legal Theory of the Greeks* (Oxford, 1956); Gerhard Thur, *Beweisfuhrung vor den Schwurgerichtshofen Athens. Die Proklesis zu Basanos* (Vienna, 1977); Louis Gernet, "Le droit pénal de la Grèce ancienne," in *Du chatiment dans la cité* (Rome, 1984), 9–35.

# 4        **Slavery and Freedom**

Jean-Paul Sartre's view that torture created two kinds of beings in twentieth-century Algeria illuminates the role of torture in the ancient Athenian state as well. He says: "Algeria cannot contain two human species, but requires a choice between them".[1] The soldiers who practiced torture on Algerian revolutionaries attempted to reduce their opponents to pure materiality, to the status of animals. Much of the debate in legal matters concerning the use of torture in ancient Athens obliquely supports a similar reading of the interrogation of the slave's body. One of the great oppositions upon which ancient culture was based differentiated slave from

---

1. Sartre, *op. cit.,* 26.

free.[2] The references to slave torture in the legal corpus indicate not only how deeply this opposition was felt, but with what difficulty free men sustained it. Free men and women could be enslaved at any time, although in Athens the Solonian reforms of the sixth century B.C.E. had ensured that Athenian citizens could not be enslaved for debt within the city-state of Attica. But prisoners of war, Greek as well as barbarian, were enslaved by their captors and often sold or ransomed. Exposed children, though born free, could live their whole lives as slaves after having been claimed from death. And slaves were often freed—by purchasing freedom with monies they were allowed to save from their own earnings, by the largesse of their owners, through wills.

Various kinds of ancient texts bear witness to the difficulty of sustaining a stable discourse on the question of slavery and freedom. Herodotos, for example, devotes attention to this issue, since one of the codes determining his history of the Persian Wars is an opposition drawn between free Greeks and barbarians enslaved to the emperor of Persia. In the *Politics* Aristotle claims that some people are slaves "by nature":

> For he is by nature [*phusei*] a slave who is capable of belonging to another (and that is why he does so belong), and who participates in reason [*logou*] so far as to apprehend it but not to possess it.
>
> (*Politics* 1254b)

Despite the authority of this statement, Aristotle nonetheless encounters problems with definition. He claims that nature intends to make the bodies of free human

---

2. On slavery, see Yvon Garlan, *Les esclaves en Grèce ancienne* (Paris, 1982).

beings and slaves different, slaves' bodies strong for service, free bodies fit for citizenship. But "as a matter of fact often the very opposite comes about—slaves have the bodies of freemen and freemen the souls only" (1254b). He points out that "to be a slave" (*douleuein*) and "slave" (*doulos*) are said *dikhôs*, "doubly, in two senses," that is, ambiguously, since there are people who are slaves not by nature (*phusis*) but by law (*nomos*). His reasoning applies to the case of noble persons captured as prisoners of war and enslaved. Aristotle recapitulates various arguments concerning slavery, and concludes temperately that in some cases natural slavery exists, cases in which it is proper and advantageous for a master to rule a slave, in some cases not.

The discourse on the use of torture in ancient Athenian law forms part of an attempt to manage the opposition between slave and free, and it betrays both need and anxiety: need to have a clear boundary between servile and free, anxiety about the impossibility of maintaining this difference. Significant for a consideration of the place of the *basanos* in the legal structure of ancient Athens is Andokides' mention of an attempt, during the Peloponnesian War, to extend torture to free citizens. The informer Diocleides had claimed that he knew who had mutilated the herms, boundary markers sacred to the god Hermes, in a famous and scandalous episode of riot and sacrilege in Athens, and had provided a list of some forty-two men.[3]

Peisander hereupon rose and moved that the decree passed in the archonship of Scamandrius be suspended and all whose names were on the list sent to

---

3. On the issue of citizen vulnerability to torture, see Gernet, "Le droit pénal," 31.

the wheel [*anabibazein epi ton trokhon*], to ensure the discovery of everyone concerned before nightfall.[4]

The Skamandrian decree apparently forbade the examination of citizens under torture. The accused were to be "caused to mount the wheel," one of the methods of torture mentioned in Aristophanes' *Frogs* (619). Peisander, a central figure in the subsequent oligarchic coup of 411, seeks here in 415 already to erase the difference between citizen and slave, to subject to torture even members of the *boulê*, the council which Peisander addresses. In fact, the council met Peisander's suggestion with shouts of approval.

> At that Mantitheus and Apsephion (among those named by Diocleides) took sanctuary on the hearth, and appealed to be allowed to furnish sureties and stand trial, instead of being racked [*mê streblôthênai*).
> (44)

The two accused council members subsequently fled to the enemy. This episode demonstrates the degree to which the incident of the mutilation of the herms shook the stability of the Athenian state, but also points to the future tendencies among the aristocratic and oligarchic parties to suspend democratic protections in a moment of crisis. The logical tendency would seem to be either to extend torture to all who could give evidence, or to forbid torture of any human being. The instability of the distinctions between slave and free, citizen and noncitizen, Greek and foreigner, becomes apparent in these debates on the possibility of state torture of citizens. Athenian citizens treasured the freedom from torture as

---

4. Andocides, *On the Mysteries* 43.

a privilege of their elevated status; Peisander's eagerness to abrogate this right is a premonition of the violence and illegality of the oligarchic coup of 411 and of the bloody rule of the Thirty after the defeat of the Athenians by the Spartans in 404.[5]

The maintenance of the distinction between slave and free is one of the matters at stake in the practice of judicial torture, and in its textualization in the literary and legal writings of the ancient city. What is the truth of the denominations *doulos,* "slave," and *eleutheros,* "free"?[6] Is it an inner truth, one given by nature, registered in the body? Or is it merely a name, an external marker devised for human convenience, by human law or custom, to justify existing social difference? The tenuousness of this difference, the instability of the status of free men and women, is rarely recognized explicitly in the texts of the ancient city. Yet the echo of such moments as Hektor's prophecy to Andromakhe on the walls of Troy in the *Iliad* persists:

> I know this thing well in my heart, and my mind
>     knows it:
> there will come a day when sacred Ilion shall
>     perish,
> and Priam, and the people of Priam of the strong
>     ash spear.

---

5. According to Cicero, the Athenians had tortured the citizen Aristogeiton in the previous century, after he and an accomplice assassinated Hipparchus, brother of the Athenian tyrant Hippias (*De partibus oratoriis,* 34).

6. On slavery, see further: Marie M. Mactoux, *Douleia: Esclavage et pratiques discursives dans l'Athènes classique* (Paris, 1980), Thomas Wiedemann, *Greek and Roman Slavery* (Baltimore, 1981), G. E. M. de Sainte-Croix, *The Class Struggle in the Ancient Greek World* (Ithaca, 1981), M. I. Finley, *Ancient Slavery*

But it is not so much the pain to come of the
    Trojans
that troubles me . . .
as troubles me the thought of you, when some
    bronze-armoured
Achaian leads you off, taking away your day of
    liberty [*eleutheron êmar*],
in tears; and in Argos you must work at the loom
    of another,
and carry water from the spring Messeis or
    Hypereia,
all unwilling, but strong will be the necessity
    [*anagkê*] upon you;
and some day seeing you shedding tears a man
    will say of you:
"This is the wife of Hektor. . . ."
So will one speak of you; and for you it will be
    yet a fresh grief,
to be widowed of such a man who could fight off
    the day of your slavery [*doulion êmar*].
                         (*Iliad* 6.447–63)

The "day of slavery" responds to the "day of freedom" as
its other. While men would be killed in battle, or in the
total destruction of a defeated city, women and children,
valuable property, became part of the booty to be divided among the victors. A woman seized in battle could
become a valued wife only to be enslaved again if her
husband fell in defeat. Xenophon recalls such scenes in
his account of the aftermath of the defeat of the Athenians by the Spartans at Aigospotamoi in 405.

As the news of the disaster was told, one man passed
it on to another, and a sound of wailing arose and

---

*and Modern Ideology* (London, 1980), Pierre Vidal-Naquet, *Le
chasseur noir: Formes de pensée et formes de société dans le
monde grec* (Paris, 1981), 211–88.

extended first from Piraeus, then along the Long Walls until it reached the city. That night no one slept. They mourned for the lost, but more still for their own fate. They thought that they themselves would now be dealt with as they had dealt with others—with the Melians, colonists of Sparta, after they had besieged and conquered Melos, with the people of Histiaea, of Scione, of Torone, of Aegina and many other states.

(Xenophon, *Hellenika* 2.2.3)

Thucydides tells us that when the Athenians defeated the Melians, who surrendered unconditionally, they put to death all the men of military age, and sold the women and children as slaves (5.116). The reversibility of fortune, of slave and free status, recurs in the imaginary of antiquity. In the Greeks' writing the possibility of unfreedom always exists, a possibility that haunts the celebration of freedom in the political, ritual ceremony that is Greek tragedy, in the writings of the ancient historians, in the work of the theorists Plato and Aristotle.

# 5                                Torture

The desire to uncover the truth of the difference between slavery and freedom constitutes part of the discourse on torture in the ancient world. Another kind of truth, what Sartre calls "the secret of everything," is named by many Greek writers as the explicit aim of judicial torture. As Louis Gernet says concerning Greek justice: "Proof is institutional; that is to say, it is derived from a system of conventions in which the signifier tends to absorb the signified."[1] In the Greek legal system, the torture of slaves figured as a guarantor of truth, as a process of truth-making.

In what context was the evidence from slave torture

---

1. Louis Gernet, *The Anthropology of Ancient Greece*, trans. John Hamilton and Blaise Nagy (Baltimore, 1981), 225–26.

presented? The earlier homicide cases about which we have knowledge were tried in the open air, to avoid pollution of the jurors by the killer; those deciding the cases belonged to aristocratic bodies of magistrates. In the fourth century, the period concerning which we have most evidence about the courts, jurors were grouped into one of the ten tribes that composed the Athenian citizenry, and then chosen at random from tribal members to serve on a jury for a particular day. Juries, or "dikasteries," as they are called, numbered from two hundred men to a maximum of six thousand, recorded in a crucial case tried in 415. Jurors received pay for their service in the courts after Perikles instituted this reform in the decade from 460 to 450. A case was required to be completed within a day at most; several private cases would be tried within a single day. The time alloted for arguments by the opponents in a trial was measured by a water-clock; the amount of water allowed for each side was determined by the seriousness of the charges. After each of the litigants spoke, brought forward witnesses, and had evidence read, the jurors placed disks or pebbles into urns to determine the winner of the suit. The parties in the case were required to speak on their own behalf, although sometimes advocates joined them. At the end of the fifth century it became customary to employ professional writers to compose one's speech for the court.[2]

Thus the scene in the court resembled the great assemblies of the democratic city, with up to six thousand men adjudicating disputes. Speakers sometimes refer to the noise of the jurors' response to their pleas; they brought their families, women and children, usually kept away from the public eye, to the court in order to influence the

---

2. On the courts, see A. R. W. Harrison, *The Law of Athens,* vol. 2, *Procedure* (Oxford, 1971), 37ff.

outcome of the trials. In this noisy, crowded scene, the speaker, like a speaker in the asssembly, spoke in his own voice to persuade his fellow citizens of his past integrity, of his connections with powerful and respected people, of his devotion to the city and her laws. He was his own witness, and he brought other witnesses with him, to confirm his view of the matters at stake but also to demonstrate his imbeddedness in a community of men and citizens, to expose his life as a man of transparent commitment to the values of the community sitting before him in judgment. In this context, the evidence from the torture of slaves is evidence from elsewhere, from another place, another body. It is evidence from outside the community of citizens, of free men. Produced by the *basanistês*, the torturer, or by the litigant in another scene, at the time of torture, such evidence differs radically from the testimony of free witnesses in the court. It is temporally estranged, institutionally, conventionally marked as evidence of another order; what is curious is that speakers again and again privilege it as belonging to a higher order of truth than that evidence freely offered in the presence of the jurors by present witnesses.

The arguments of the legal orators claim that truth is what is at stake in the *basanos*. Demosthenes, for example, speaks of the reliability of evidence obtained under torture:

Now, you consider *basanos* the most reliable of all tests both in private and in public affairs. Wherever slaves and free men are present and facts have to be found, you do not use the statements of the free witnesses, but you seek to discover the truth [*tên alêtheian*] by applying *basanos* to the slaves. Quite properly, men of the jury, since witnesses have sometimes been found not to have given true evidence [*talêthê*], whereas no statements made as a result of *basanos* have ever been proved to be untrue.[3]

There are many such passages. The slave body has become, in the democratic city, the site of torture and of the production of truth.

The argument concerning the greater value of slave evidence frequently occurs in accusations against an opponent who has refused to allow his slaves to be tortured. The speaker claims then that this failure to produce slave witnesses proves indirectly that their testimony would condemn their owner. Isaios uses similar language to that of Demosthenes to accuse, demonstrating how such arguments become a commonplace of forensic rhetoric (8.12). Although elsewhere in the judicial corpus we find the recognition of the possibility of tainted evidence from torture, here Demosthenes presents the baldest justifications for torture, the most absolute claim that torture, unlike the free and uncompelled testimony of free men, produces truth.

In a speech of Lykourgos against Leokrates, the torture of slaves becomes a crucial matter for debate. Lykourgos has accused Leokrates of treason because he deserted Athens after the battle of Chaeronea (338), defying a decree of the citizens. In this same oration, Leokrates recalls the murder of Phrynikhos, who was one of the oligarchic conspirators of the coup in Athens in 411, and the finding that Phrynikhos had been engaged in treachery, that his murderers had been unjustly imprisoned. The investigation of the murder involved the use of torture to clarify what had happened. "The people noted what had happened and, releasing the prisoners, held an inquiry after torture [*basanôn genomenôn apekrine*]" (112). Phrynikhos, the dead man, was tried, found

---

3. Demosthenes 30.37.

guilty, his bones dug up and cast out of Attica. Much earlier, Thucydides had described this same event in his account of the oligarchic coup of 411, saying that the accomplice of Phrynikhos' murderer, an Argive, was arrested and put to the torture (*basanizomenos;* 8.92). The Greek syntax in the speech of Lykourgos in the law court allows for an especially disembodied and alienated representation of this torture; the genitive absolute form effaces both the agent of the torture and its logical relationship to the rest of the sentence: "tortures having taken place, tortures having happened."

Lykourgos argues against Leokrates that he submitted to the defense a written challenge, and demanded the slaves of Leokrates for torture (*basanizein*), "according to the right procedure for making challenges" (28). He asks in the courtroom that the challenge be read. He continues:

Every one of you knows that in matters of dispute it is considered by far the just and most democratic [*dêmotikôtaton*] course, when there are male or female slaves, who possess the necessary information, to examine these by torture and so have facts to go upon instead of hearsay, particularly when the case concerns the public and is of vital interest to the state. Certainly I cannot be called unjust in my prosecution of Leocrates. I was even willing at my own risk to let the proof rest on the torture of his male and female slaves, but the defendant, realizing his guilt, rejected the offer instead of accepting it. And yet, gentlemen, the male and female slaves of Leocrates would have been far readier to deny any of the real facts than to invent lies against their master.[4]

. . . . . .

---

4. Lycurgus, *Against Leocrates,* 29–31.

Which people could not have been misled by cunning or a deceptive argument? The male and female slaves. Naturally [*kata physin*], when tortured, they would have told the whole truth [*pasan tên alêtheian*] about all the offences.[5]

He argues that by nature the tortured slaves would have told the truth; does this mean that any human being, when tortured, will produce the truth, or that it is the nature of slaves to tell the truth under torture? Free citizen men will be deceived by clever arguments; slaves by nature will not be misled because they think with their bodies. Slaves are bodies; citizens possess *logos*, reason.

The use of the word *dêmotikôtaton* in this context is particularly intriguing; the word means most "popular, democratic," that is, as opposed to an elitist, aristocratic course. This appeal to the practice of torture as an integral and valued part of the legal machinery of the democracy points up the contradictory nature of Athenian democracy, and the ways in which the application of the democratic reforms of Athens were carefully limited to the lives of male citizens, and intrinsic to the production and justification of this notion of male citizenship.

The infamous episodes of the profanation of the Eleusinian Mysteries and of the mutilation of the herms, mentioned earlier, generated several court cases in which *basanos* figures. The herms were bronze or marble pillars topped with a bust, often depicting the god Hermes, and adorned with male genitals; they stood everywhere in the streets of Athens. One night in 415, just before the departure of an Athenian expedition for Sicily, unknown revelers mutilated these boundary markers. In the course of the investigation of these acts

---

5. Ibid., 32.

of sacrilege, the Athenians discovered that parodic en-
actments of the mysteries of Demeter and Kore had also
been carried out in Athens. Among those implicated was
Alkibiades, the brilliant ward of Perikles who had advocated the expedition to Sicily (Thucydides 6.27–29).

In a defense speech of another of those accused, Andokides, forced to defend himself many years later against
the accusation of involvement in these acts of impiety,
the defendant recalls the use of torture in an earlier
defense. He says that he had opposed the plan to mutilate
the herms, but when he was thrown from a horse and
disabled, one of the conspirators had told the others he
was part of their plot. He had denied participation in the
conspiracy and says, "I supported this account [literally,
*hôs oun ên taut'alêthê*, "that these things were true"] by
handing over my slave for torture [*basanisai*], to prove
that I was ill at the time in question and had not even left
my bed."[6] Among other such passages, this one suggests
definitively that such incidents of torture did actually
take place, rather than being merely hypothetical possi-
bilities in the spectrum of legal argument.

Antiphon (480–411), a citizen of strong aristocratic
allegiance, like Peisander and Phrynikhos participated
in the coup of 411 and was executed for his part in that
conspiracy after the oligarchic government fell.[7] Some
of the orations attributed to Antiphon are apparently
oratorical exercises, examples of how courtroom
speeches should be composed. In one of the show pieces
in what is called the First Tetralogy, the speaker addresses the matter of evidence derived from torture. This
set of four speeches was probably composed to instruct
either those litigants who appeared in court, or the *logo-
graphoi*, writers hired to compose *logoi*, "speeches," for

---

6. Andocides, *On the Mysteries*, 64.
7. See Thucydides 8.68.

those involved in trials, who were themselves required always to deliver before the jury their speeches of accusation or defense.

These four speeches present an argument, a response, a counter argument and a counter response. The matter of a slave's evidence is crucial to the case. The second speaker, defending himself against a murder charge, wants to deny the accuracy of testimony obtained from a murdered man's slave attendant who himself died from the assault, since this testimony, although not obtained under torture, implicates the defendant:

> Why should the evidence of the attendant be allowed any weight? In his terror at the peril in which he stood, there was no likelihood of his recognizing the murderers. On the other hand, it was likely enough that he would obediently confirm any suggestions made by his masters. We distrust the evidence of slaves in general, or we should not torture [*an ebasanizomen*] them; so what justification have you for putting me to death on the evidence of this one?
>
> (ii, b, 7)[8]

Here we see the often-repeated argument that the evidence of slaves is regarded as truthful only when exacted through torture; the hearsay evidence obtained from this slave while he lived cannot be considered trustworthy and truthful, since it was testimony given while the slave lay free from duress. In the next speech, an answer to this one, the opposing speaker refutes the line of argument concerning the dead man's status:

> The defence are wrong when they say that the evidence of the slave is not to be trusted; where evidence of this

---

8. *Minor Attic Orators: Antiphon, Andocides*, trans. K. J. Maidment (Cambridge, Mass., 1941).

sort is concerned, slaves are not tortured: they are given their freedom. It is when they deny a theft or conspire with their masters to keep silence that we believe them to tell the truth only under torture.

(ii, g, 4)

The slave in question here, since he presumably bravely defended his master and was mortally wounded in that defense, is assumed to be virtually free, since a grateful master would have freed him. Therefore his evidence, not obtained under torture, should be accepted as that of a free man, and therefore as true.

    This argument is in its turn refuted in the last speech of the First Tetralogy:

Why should the evidence of the slave be thought more trustworthy than that of free men? Free men are disfranchised and fined, should their evidence be considered false; whereas this slave, who gave us no opportunity of either cross-examining or torturing him—when can he be punished? No, when can he be cross-examined?

(ii, d, 7)

This whole set of arguments, presumably composed as an exemplary exchange in a hypothetical debate, lays out the spectrum of arguments concerning slave testimony under torture. Although the two speakers disagree about the status of the testimony of the deceased slave, their argument rests on whether the man should be considered slave or free at the time of his identification of the murderer. If the jurors believe him virtually free, his evidence stands, given freely and truthfully as that of a freed and therefore free and truthful man. If they consider him still servile at the time of his death, then his evidence is worthless as testimony derived from a slave in an unreliable manner, that is, without the benefit of torture. Neither speaker in this debate questions the conventional wisdom that truth can only be obtained from a free man in free testimony, or from a slave under torture.

In another speech attributed to Antiphon, this one part of a case presumably actually tried, torture again plays an important role in the defense of a man accused of murder, Euxitheos. In this trial also, the issue of the torturability of the slave occupies the speaker's attention. One of the witnesses tortured was not a slave but a free man, not a Greek but a foreigner of some sort. Here the orator wants the jury to assume that the testimony of a free man, though obtained under torture, is more reliable than that of a tortured slave. The speaker for the defense seeks to discredit the testimony of the slave by claiming that a delay occurred before he was tortured, and that in the interval the slave was promised his freedom:

> Probably both of these considerations induced him to make the false charges against me which he did; he hoped to gain his freedom, and his one immediate wish was to end the torture. I need not remind you, I think, that witnesses under torture are biased in favour of those who do most of the torturing; they will say anything likely to gratify them. It is their one chance of salvation, especially when the victims of their lies happen not to be present. Had I myself proceeded to give orders that the slave should be racked [*strebloun*] for not telling the truth, that step in itself would doubtless have been enough to make him stop incriminating me falsely.
>
> (5.31–32)

The speaker, because for once forced to confront the evidence of a tortured slave, rather than bemoaning the lack of slave evidence, here points out the absolute unreliability of slave evidence, based as it is on the will of the torturer. Bizarrely, however, he ends by claiming that the true truth would have emerged, another truth truer than the first, if he himself had been the torturer. The defendant may be distinguishing, perhaps ironically, between the "truth" of what is told—a statement— and the "truth" of a context, a relationship of power, in which the first truth is told. If so, it is interesting that the defendant distinguishes between an essentialist notion of truth and a pragmatic notion of truth in the case of the slave, but not in the case of the free foreigner, where a reversion to the essentialist notion appears to occur. And the logic he exposes, that the slave will say anything to gratify his torturer, is dropped as soon as he himself becomes the torturer. We can imagine the body of the slave ripped apart in a tug-of-war between two litigants, in a law case in which he was implicated only by proximity.

This very slave, who had been purchased by the prosecution, in fact later changed his testimony, according to the speaker because he recognized his imminent doom. Nonetheless the prosecution put him to death. The defendant continues:

> Clearly, it was not his person, but his evidence, which they required; had the man remained alive, he would have been tortured by me in the same way, and the prosecution would be confronted with their plot: but once he was dead, not only did the loss of his person mean that I was deprived of my opportunity of establishing the truth, but his false statements are assumed to be true.
>
> (5.35)

All of the prosecution's case rests on the testimony of the tortured and now dead slave; the defendant claims to be completely frustrated, since now the truth lies in a realm inaccessible to him. He cannot torture the dead man and discover the "real" truth. Even though the slave had at first insisted on the defendant's innocence, he had under torture called him guilty:

> At the start, before being placed on the wheel [*trok-hon*], in fact, until extreme pressure was brought to bear, the man adhered to the truth [*alêtheia*] and declared me innocent. It was only when on the wheel, and when driven to it, that he falsely incriminated me, in order to put an end to the torture.
>
> (5.40–41)

The persistence of the defendant's desire *himself* to torture this slave claims our attention; even after the inevitability of false testimony under torture stands exposed, he bemoans the retreat of the slave into the realm of the untorturable, of the dead.

> I repeat, let no one cause you to forget that the prosecution put the informer to death, that they used every effort to prevent his appearance in court and to make it impossible for me to take him and examine him under torture on my return. . . . Instead, they bought the slave and put him to death, entirely on their own initiative [*idia*].
>
> (5.46–47)

In this same case, another witness, not a slave, also underwent torture. This man is free, but apparently not Greek, since he too was tortured:

> Then there was the second man. He had travelled on the same boat as I: had been present throughout the voyage: and had been constantly in my company. When tortured in the same way, he confirmed the first

and last statements of the other as true; for he declared
me innocent from start to finish.

(5.42)

This aspect of the case is especially revealing, since the
defendant claims that this free man (*eleutheros*, 5.49)
continued to tell the truth, even under torture.

> In spite of similar torture [*têi autêi basanôi basanizo-
> menos*], the free man has not even yet said anything to
> damage me. He could not be influenced by offers of
> freedom, as his companion had been; and at the same
> time he was determined to cling to the truth, cost what
> it might.
>
> (5.49–50)

The free man knew that the torture would end; he also
could not be bribed by promises of freedom for giving
the answers the torturers desired to hear. In this case,
the defendant gives priority to the free man's unfree
testimony; unlike the free testimony of an Athenian in a
courtroom, this evidence was derived from torture, but
the defendant seeks to give it the added authority of the
free man in spite of its origin in this procedure tainted
with unfreedom, because it supports his view of the case.

Another mention of *basanos*, where the word means
torture of slaves as opposed to "scrutiny," for example,
of a citizen's testimony, comes in a poisoning case; Antiphon refers to a previous trial in which a slave was
accused, tortured, and executed for murder; the speaker,
pronouncing a speech supposedly written for him by
Antiphon, as was customary in the court, now accuses
his stepmother, the murdered man's wife, of the poisoning. The accuser points out that he had asked for permission to torture the defendant's slaves; the defense had
refused to hand them over. He suggests that their denial
of permission amounts to an admission of guilt (1.6–12).

He then recalls the circumstances of the earlier murder trial, in which the mistress of Philoneos was accused of single-handedly plotting the murder which the accuser now claims was in fact plotted by his stepmother. He says that the mistress thought the poison she administered was a love potion. Two men died on consuming it.

> In atonement, the subordinate who carried out the deed has been punished as she deserved, although the crime in no sense originated from her: she was broken on the wheel [*trokhistheisa*] and handed over to the executioner.
>
> (1.20)

The mistress was obviously a slave or non-Athenian, liable to torture, the *basanos* of the "wheel." The accuser shows pity neither concerning the torture nor concerning the execution of this slave who innocently, as he acknowledges, gave what she believed to be a love philter to her lover and his friend, the accuser's father. This indifference provides evidence for the Greeks' notions of guilt and responsibility. Although the woman had no *intention* of killing her master. as the instrument of his death she was responsible for it and therefore liable first to torture and then to execution.

In a case called "On the Choreutes," probably delivered some time around 412 B.C.E., Antiphon again makes the distinction between slave and free testimony:

> Let him go to the persons who had been present at the accident . . . and let him interrogate and cross-examine [*elegkhein*] them. Let him question the free men as befitted free men; for their own sakes and in the interest of justice, they would give a faithful account [*talêthê*] of what had occurred. As to the slaves, if he considered that they were answering his questions truthfully, well and good; if he did not, I was ready to

place all my own at his disposal for examination under torture, and should he demand any that did not belong to me, I agreed to obtain the consent of their owner and hand them over to him to examine as he liked.

(6.23)

In this case, as in many others, the opposition refuses this challenge, and the speaker seeks to use this fact to condemn his opponent. He further justifies his claims by reminding his audience of the various compulsions involved in these inquiries:

You do not need to be reminded, gentlemen, that the one occasion when compulsion [*anagkai*] is as absolute and as effective as is humanly possible, and when the rights of a case are ascertained thereby most surely and most certainly, arises when there is an abundance of witnesses, both slave and free, and it is possible to put pressure [*anagkazein*] upon the free men by exacting an oath or word of honour, the most solemn and the most awful form of compulsion known to free men, and upon the slaves by other devices [*heterais anagkais*], which will force them to tell the truth even if their revelations are bound to cost them their lives, as the compulsion of the moment [*hê gar parousa anagkê*] has a stronger influence over each than the fate which he will suffer by compulsion afterwards.

(6.25)

That is, the free man is compelled by oaths; he might lose his rights as a citizen if he lied under oath. The slave, even though he will certainly be put to death as a consequence of what he reveals under torture, will nonetheless, under torture, reveal the truth. The two kinds of compulsion are equated, one appropriate for the free man, one for the slave.

Torture serves not only to exact a truth, some truth or

other, which will benefit one side of the case or the other. It also functions as a gambit in the exchange between defendant and prosecution; if for any reason one of them refuses to give up slaves to torture, the other can claim that the missing testimony would of a certainty support his view of things. And as I argued earlier, torture also serves to mark the boundary between slave and free beings. Torture can be enacted against free, non-Greek beings as well as slaves; all "barbarians" are assimilated to slaves. Slaves are barbarians, barbarians are slaves; all are susceptible to torture. Torturability creates a difference which is naturalized. And even the sophistry of the First Tetralogy, which wants to create a category of virtually free in the case of the slave who would have been freed had he lived, seeks to support this division of human beings into free, truth-telling creatures, and torturable slave/barbarians, who will only produce truth on the wheel.

# 6 The Slave's Truth

Torture performs at least two functions in the Athenian state. As an instrument of demarcation, it delineates the boundary between slave and free, between the untouchable bodies of free citizens and the torturable bodies of slaves. The ambiguity of slave status, the difficulty of sustaining an absolute sense of differences, is addressed through this practice of the state, which carves the line between slave and free on the bodies of the unfree. In the work of the wheel, the rack, and the whip, the torturer carries out the work of the *polis;* citizen is made distinct from noncitizen, Greek from barbarian, slave from free. The practice of *basanos* administers to the anxiety about enslavement, hauntingly evoked in the texts of Athenian tragedy that recall the fall of cities, particularly the fall of Troy, evoked as well in the histories that recount Athenian destruction of subject allies.

We should remember that the rule that tragedy should not address contemporary events was established in part because of the overwhelming impact on the Athenian audience of Phrynikhos's tragedy on the taking of Miletus by the Persians in 494; Herodotos recalls: "most of the men were killed by the Persians . . . the women and children were made slaves [*en andrapodôn logôi eginonto*]" (6.19). He goes on: "The Athenians . . . showed their profound distress at the capture of Miletus in a number of ways, and in particular, when Phrynichus produced his play, *The Capture of Miletus*, the audience in the theatre burst into tears. The author was fined a thousand drachmae for reminding them of a disaster which touched them so closely, and they forebade anybody ever to put the play on the stage again" (6.21). Tragedy rarely again directly represented such sufferings, except in Aeschylus's *Persians*, in which only the Athenians' enemies experienced humiliation and defeat. The text of Herodotos depicts the enslavement of whole cities. The citizens of fifth-century Athens, especially in time of war, must have feared for their own safety and the integrity of their status as free men and women, and were evidently disquieted by the dramatic representation of the erasure of the boundary between free persons and slaves.

But the desire to clarify the respective status of slave and free is not the motive, never the explicit motive, of torture. Rather, again and again, even in the face of arguments discounting evidence derived from torture, speakers in the courts describe the *basanos* as a search for truth. How is this possible? And how are the two desires related? The claim is made that truth resides in the slave body.

Isaios uses language almost identical to that of Demosthenes to claim that torture provides truth:

You Athenians hold the opinion that both in public
and in private matters examination under torture [*basanon*] is the most searching test; and so, when you
have slaves and free men before you, and it is necessary
that some contested point should be cleared up, you
do not employ the evidence of free men but seek to
establish the truth [*heurein tên alêtheian*] by putting
the slaves to torture [*tous doulous basanizontes*]. This
is a perfectly reasonable course, for you are well aware
that before now witnesses have appeared not to be
giving true evidence [*talêthê marturêsai*], whereas no
one who has been examined under torture [*tôn de ba-
sanisthentôn oudenes*] has ever been convicted of giving false evidence as the result of being tortured [*hôs
ouk alêthê ek tôn basanôn eipontes*].[1]

The evidence derived from the slave's body and reported
to the court, evidence from the past, is considered superior to that given freely in the court, before the jury, in
the presence of the litigants.

Aristotle says, in distinguishing among master, slave,
and animal:

He is by nature a slave who is capable of belonging to
another (and that is why he does so belong), and who
participates in reason so far as to apprehend [*ais-
thanesthai*] it but not to possess [*ekhein*] it; for the
animals other than man are subservient not to reason,
by apprehending it, but to feelings. (*Politics* 1254b)

That is, the master possesses reason, *logos*. When giving
evidence in court, he knows the difference between truth
and falsehood, he can reason and produce true speech,
*logos*, and he can reason about the consequences of false-

---

1. Isaios 8.12.

hood, the deprivation of his rights as a citizen. The slave, on the other hand, possessing not reason, but rather a body strong for service (*iskhura pros tên anagkaian khrêsin*), must be forced to utter the truth, which he can apprehend, although not possessing reason as such. Unlike an animal, a being that possesses only feelings, and therefore can neither apprehend reason, *logos*, nor speak, *legein*, the slave can testify when his body is tortured because he recognizes reason without possessing it himself.

What kind of truth is the slave's truth? Aristotle says of the relationship between slave and master:

> The slave is a part of the master—he is, as it were, a part of the body, alive [*empsukhon ti*] but yet separated [*kekhôrismenon*] from it. (*Politics* 1255b)

Thus, according to Aristotle's logic, representative or not, the slave's truth is the master's truth; it is in the body of the slave that the master's truth lies, and it is in torture that his truth is revealed. The torturer reaches through the master to the slave's body, and extracts the truth from it. The master can conceal the truth, since he possesses reason and can choose between truth and lie, can choose the penalty associated with false testimony. His own point of vulnerability is the body of his slave, which can be compelled not to lie, can be forced to produce the truth. If he decides to deny the body of his slave to the torturer, assumptions will be made that condemn him.

In his *Rhetoric*, addressed to an audience requiring instruction in techniques of persuasion, Aristotle discusses the value of torture as evidence in forensic rhetoric. It appears in his list of "inartificial proofs," *atekhnôn pisteôn*, that is to say, proofs made not through the art of rhetoric, but adduced from a realm outside of the speaker's invention: "all those which have not been furnished by ourselves but were already in existence."

(1355b). In contrast, "artificial proofs," *entekhnoi*, are "all that can be constructed by system and by our own efforts." While "artful," "artificial" proofs must be invented, and Aristotle provides guidelines for their production, "artless," "inartificial" proofs come from elsewhere, are brought in to be used in argument. His list includes laws, witnesses, contracts, and oaths, as well as torture (1375a).

> Torture is a kind of evidence, which appears trustworthy, because a sort of compulsion is attached to it. Nor is it difficult to see what may be said concerning it, and by what arguments, if it is in our favour, we can exaggerate its importance by asserting that it is the only true kind of evidence; but if it is against us and in favour of our opponent, we can destroy its value by telling the truth [*talêthê*] about all kinds of torture generally; for those under compulsion are as likely to give false evidence as true, some being ready to endure everything rather than tell the truth, while others are equally ready to make false charges against others, in the hope of being sooner released from torture. It is also necessary to be able to quote actual examples of the kind with which the judges are acquainted. It may also be said that evidence given under torture is not true [*hôs ouk eisin alêtheis hai basanoi*]; for many thick-witted and thick-skinned persons, and those who are stout-hearted heroically hold out under sufferings, while the cowardly and cautious, before they see the sufferings before them, are bold enough; wherefore evidence from torture may be considered utterly untrustworthy.
>
> (*Rhetoric* 1376b–1377a)

Aristotle advocates the pragmatic approach; one can argue either side concerning the truth of torture. The weight of Aristotle's exposition lies on the falsity of evidence produced under torture, either because he believes it to be more likely false, or because speakers in the court are more likely to claim its truth, and therefore those he is instructing, if faced with evidence from torture, need assistance in refuting its claims. If we heed Demosthenes' and Isaios's claim that no evidence from torture was ever proven false, we see the difficulty of the litigant faced with slave torture. It appears that common wisdom attributed a superior value to the evidence of a tortured slave, a value weighted above that of the free man, and that Aristotle must labor on behalf of his readers to counter the weight of evidence from this privileged source. Like laws, oaths, contracts and witnesses, proof by torture comes from somewhere else, from outside the text of the speaker in the lawsuit.

The very ambiguity of evidence derived from torture, an ambiguity that Aristotle recognizes and accounts for, replicates the ambiguity of social status on which it depends. Slave is only circumstantially differentiable from free; truth in the lawcourt can only provisionally and polemically be distinguished from falsehood. The two issues are linked in the body of the tortured, who on the rack, on the wheel, under the whip assumes a relationship to truth. Truth is constituted as residing in the body of the slave; because he can apprehend reason, without possessing reason, under coercion he is assumed to speak the truth. The free man, the citizen, because he possesses reason, can lie freely, recognizing that he may lose his rights, but choosing to gamble that his authority will authorize his speech. The slave, incapable of reasoning, can only produce truth under coercion, can produce only truth under coercion. The court assumes that he will lie unless compelled by physical force to speak truly and that when compelled he will speak truly. As Gernet says, "Proof is institutional." Proof, and therefore truth, are constituted by the Greeks as best found in the evidence derived from torture. Truth, *alêtheia*, comes from elsewhere, from another place, from the place of the other.

# 7    Torture and Writing

The tortured body retains scars, marks that recall the violence inflicted upon it by the torturer. In part because slaves were often tattooed in the ancient world, such marks of torture resonate in the Greek mind with tattoos, and with other forms of metaphorical inscription, in Greek thinking considered analogous to writing on the body.[1] I have discussed the topos of corporeal inscription elsewhere. The woman's body was in ancient Greece sometimes likened to a writing tablet, a surface to be

---

1. On Kafka, contemporary torture, and writing on the body, see Michel DeCerteau, "Corps torturés, paroles capturées," *Cahiers pour un temps*, special edition on Michel DeCerteau, ed. Luce Giard (Paris, 1987), 61–70.

"ploughed," inscribed by the hand, the plough, the penis of her husband and master.[2]

One especially intriguing mention of slave tattooing occurs in Herodotos's *Histories*, in a narrative in which the possibility of torture remains implicit. Although I have discussed this episode elsewhere, I want here to draw out its implications for a consideration of the relationship between torture and truth. Histiaios of Miletus sends a message urging revolt to a distant ally by shaving the head of his most trusted slave, tattooing the message on the slave's head, then waiting for the slave's hair to grow back. He sends the slave on his journey, ordering him to say at the journey's end only that the "destinataire," the receiver of the message, should shave off his hair and look at his head. The message reaches its goal, and Aristagoras the receiver revolts (Herodotos, *Histories* 5.35).

The tattooed head is a protection against torture. If the slave were captured and tortured, he would not himself know the message of revolt. He could not betray his master if questioned and interrogated specifically about his master's intentions to rise up against those who have enslaved him. He did not know the content of Histiaios' communication with Aristagoras. But he did know the instructions he bore to Aristagoras, to shave his head and read the message inscribed there. The ruse only displaces the discovery of the message's truth by a single step, but in this case it succeeds in protecting the message. Here the tattooing, the inscription on the slave's body, subverts the intention of torture to expose the truth.

In other contexts in ancient Greece, slave tattooing

---

2. See P. duBois, *Sowing the Body: Psychoanalysis and Ancient Representations of Women* (Chicago, 1988), chap. 7, "Tablet," 130–66.

serves as a sort of label. It is as if writing on the slave body indicated the contents of that body. Such a function of writing recalls the work of Denise Schmandt-Besserat, who argues that writing originates in the markings on the outside of packages recording their contents.[3] Aristotle points out in the *Politics*, as we have seen, that the slave body ought to reveal its truth, ought to be immediately perceptible as a servile body to the eye, but in fact sometimes it is not. A tattoo on a slave reveals his or her true status. In Aristophanes' *Babylonians*, of which only fragments remain, we learn that prisoners of war were sometimes branded or inscribed with a mark indicating the city they served.[4]

The torture of slaves appears in several suggestive contexts in the work of Herodes, a comic writer of the third century B.C.E. The second mime, a parody of a forensic speech like those discussed earlier, presents a mock lawcourt scene, in which Battaros the brothelkeeper addresses a jury, bringing a complaint against a certain Thales who he claims assaulted one of his Tyrian prostitutes. As part of his accusation against Thales, Battaros offers himself up for torture:

If all Thales wanted was to beat up
A poor slave and wants her to testify
Under torture [*basanon*], then I will take her place
   [literally, put me on the rack, *streblou me*].

---

3. D. Schmandt-Besserat, "An Archaic Recording System and the Origin of Writing," *Syro-Mesopotamian Studies* 1 (1977), 31–70; "The Earliest Precursor of Writing," *Scientific American* 238, no.6 (June 1978), 50–59; "An Archaic Recording System in the Uruk-Jemdet Nasr Period," *American Journal of Archaeology* 83 (1979), 19–48.

4. Schol. on Aristophanes fr. 64; Apostol. 15.32, p. 636.

Willingly! But he must pay just the same
If he hurts me, just as if I were her.
Did Minos balance this case on his scales,
Could he try it a better way than this?
      (Herondas, *Mime* 2.87–91)[5]

Battaros offers himself to be racked, provided that he will be reimbursed for his trouble. He is a metic, a resident alien in Cos; his vulnerability to torture may be questionable. If the law is like Athens', he could not be tortured as a nonslave unless the safety of the state was believed to be at stake. His offer may be an empty one, a comic appeal to the imaginary jury trying this case. The torture, he may be suggesting, is just another form of physical attention for which he will be rewarded by winning the court's award, just as he receives money for one of his girls, or for offering his own body to a client.

The fifth mime establishes a connection among writing, tattooing, punishment, and torture. It represents a scene between Bitinna, mistress of her house, and Gastron (a pun on belly, or appetite), her slave and lover. The mistress accuses the slave of infidelity with another woman. She blames herself for setting him *en anthrôpois* (15), "among human beings", but she promises to mend her ways and return him to his servile position. The slave begs forgiveness, vows never again to do wrong; if he does, he says, she should tattoo him: *stixon* (28). She commands that he be taken to "the abode of torment," *zêtreion* (32), and be given a thousand lashes on his back, a thousand on his belly.

The slave-girl runs after, to recall him before he reaches *tas anagkas* (59), "the torments." The mistress has decided upon tattooing as a punishment, rather than

_____

5. *The Mimes of Herondas*, trans. Guy Davenport (San Francisco, 1981), 12.

flogging, and summons Kosis the tattooer to come with needles and ink. Although the slave girl begs for mercy, Bitinna says:

> Am I to let be this slave of slaves? Who then that encountered me would not rightly spit in my face? No, by the Queen, since, though he is a human being, he does not know himself, soon he will know, having this inscription on his forehead.
>
> (74–79)[6]

Herodes invokes the inscription at Delphi, also cited by Plato: *gnôthi seauton*, "Know yourself."[7] This slave, who has lost sight of his position as slave by having sex with another besides his mistress, will be reminded of his status, reminded to know himself as slave.

This placement of the "epigram," whatever it is, if it is that, on the *metope*, the forehead of the slave, makes the inscription a sign. The message of Herodotos's slave was concealed by his hair, directed to a specified other, the recipient who received the slave as a vehicle for his master's words. The communication was not directed to the slave himself. In the case of Herodes' slave, the man named "Belly" would bear a sign meant to remind him of his humble status. A man spared the thousands of lashes desired by his mistress, he remained liable to marking by her as her property. His tattoo would be a sign of her possession, her ability to control his body as she wished, to use him exclusively for her sexual gratifi-

---

6. *The Characters of Theophrastus. Herodes, Cercidas and the Greek Choliambic Poets (Except Callimachus and Babrius)*, rev. ed., trans. J. M. Edmonds and A. D. Knox (Cambridge, Mass., 1946).

7. See Herodas, *Mimiambi*, ed. I. C. Cunningham (Oxford, 1971), 159.

cation, to inscribe him as she desired. And the inscription would also be a message to his presumed other lover, who would read on his body the sign of his belonging to another. If the inscription read "Know yourself," it would speak to anyone who gazed at the slave's forehead, directing the viewer to know himself or herself as slave or free person, as owner of this slave, or not. And after all, after the slave-girl's appeals, the mistress spares the slave both whipping and tattooing; his punishment is to be only that he must drink unhoneyed wine, perhaps an allusion to a sexual act to be performed on his mistress, in greater likelihood a reference to bitter feast days henceforward.

The mime reveals some aspects of daily life of the third century, gives a flavor of the absolute authority of a slave's owner, of the intimacy of slaves and mistress in an ordinary household. The mistress writes her message on the slave's body; he is a mere vehicle for her word, after having been thoroughly silenced earlier in the poem. The mime does not refer to torture, although it does address the matter of truth, in a sense, the truth of identity, of the radical distinction between freedom and slavery. This slave is to be punished rather than tortured; his lashes would be performed by a specialist in the field, an expert at the disciplining of slaves. The mime does not describe a judicial, legal torture for evidence. But the substitution of tattooing for whipping argues for the vulnerability of the slave's body, which would carry an imperative upon it, a reminder of difference, of the line between slavery and freedom.

# 8  Buried Truth

If torture helped to manage the troublesome differentiation between slave and free in the ancient city, it also served as a redundant practice reinforcing the dominant notion of the Greeks that truth was an inaccessible, buried secret. In his valuable book *Les maîtres de vérité dans la Grèce archaïque*, Marcel Detienne describes a historical shift in the Greeks' ideas about truth that corresponds to the historical shift from mythic to rational thought.[1] According to Detienne, *Alêtheia* is at first conceived of by the Greeks in an ambiguous relationship with *Lêthê*, forgetting; truth is the possession of the poet and the just king, who has access to this truth through

---

1. Marcel Detienne, *Les maîtres de vérité dans la Grèce archaïque*, 2d ed. (Paris, 1973).

memory. *Alêtheia* is caught up in a relationship of ambiguity with *Lêthê* because, for example, the poet who speaks truth by using memory also confers truth's other, forgetfulness, oblivion of pain and sorrow, on his listeners. His "magico-religious" speech, as Detienne calls it, which exists in an ambiguous relationship with truth, persists as the dominant form in the Greek world until the speech of warriors, the citizens who form the city's phalanxes, a speech of dialogue, comes to dominate the social world in the time of the *polis*. Detienne associates a resultant secularization of poetic *Alêtheia* with the name of the poet Simonides. *Doxa*, seeming, becomes the rival province of sophistic and rhetorical speech, while *Alêtheia* comes to belong to an unambiguously "philosophico-religious" domain. In this field of discourse the logic of ambiguity typical of the *Alêtheia-Lêthê* relationship is replaced by a logic of contradiction, in which *Alêtheia* is opposed to *Apatê*, deception, as its other. The common use of memory provides a link between these two stages of thinking truth; the secularization of speech marks a break between a mythic and a rationalist semantic field in which the term *Alêtheia* persists.

This account of the social evolution of the term *truth* has significance for my study, even though, as Detienne himself would acknowledge today, the notion of a radical historical break between a time of myth and a time of reason has been called into question. While I accept the terms of Detienne's description of the change in the definition of the semantic field into which *Alêtheia* falls from the time of Hesiod to that of the sophists, one category that seems lacking from his analysis is that of gender. I want to articulate the gender marking of the term *alêtheia* and its relationship to the *basanos* that reveals truth. Gender seems crucial especially to the "logic of ambiguity" by which *Alêtheia* is related to *Lêthê*. In addition, the philosophical term truth has its neglected judi-

cial aspect and borders the ways in which truth is implicated in ascertaining guilt and innocence in the courts
of the city. To supplement the histories of "truth," I have
already considered the judicial form of truth. In this
chapter, I want to mark the sources of this truth, the
truth of *Alêtheia* as ambiguously opposed to *Lêthê*, so as
to see if the emergence of truth from oblivion, the location of truth as something to be uncovered from oblivion
through memory, can be associated with sexual difference.

The dominant spatial model for the approach to truth
appears to be the descent. In his work on the terms
*nous* and *nostos* in Homer, Douglas Frame describes
the journey of Odysseus to the land of the dead, to his
encounter with his mother, the various heroes, and with
Teiresias, pointing out that the journey is marked by the
ancient association between descent into darkness and
re-emergence into light. The journey of the hero com-
prises a death and symbolic rebirth; his acquisition of
*nous*, "mind," is contingent on his descent. The pattern
of the journey to knowledge resembles that of Gilgamesh
in the Near Eastern epic that bears his name, and is
echoed in other cultural practices in ancient Greece.
Prophetic figures like Teiresias and Amphiaraos, poets,
and the consultants of oracles all penetrate an invisible
world. The ritual consultation of the oracle of Trophonios, for example, involves a descent into the earth, a
symbolic death, and a rebirth with uncommon knowledge.[2] Detienne describes the Trophonios oracle:

La descente dans l'Hadès du consultant de Trophonios
est donc comme le répondant rituel de l'expérience

---

2. See Marcel Detienne, *Les maîtres*, 45–47. See also duBois,
*Sowing the Body*.

religieuse par laquelle le devin ou le poète inspiré
pénètre dans le monde invisible.

(47)

Detienne seems to efface the possibility that this descent
had association with a return or an entry into what the
Greeks saw as the female body of the earth. Traditionally, the invisible world of Earth that lies beneath the
surface of the earth, in the space of burial, was associated
with the mother, with the woman's body. As a vessel, a
container, a body filled with an interiority itself full of
potential for holding, for entreasuring or warming, the
woman's body was seen as analogous to the earth, with
its caves, crevasses, openings into an invisible world
from which the living emerged, into which the dead
departed.

What is the relationship of Lethe to this gendered landscape? In the *Odyssey,* the hero Odysseus receives guidance about his journey to the land of the dead from the
enchantress Circe. Having mounted the "surpassingly
beautiful bed of Circe," he hears from her:

> . . .when you have crossed with your ship the
>     stream of the Ocean, you will
> find there a thickly wooded shore, and the groves
>     of Persephone,
> and tall black poplars growing, and fruit-
>     perishing willows;
> then beach your ship on the shore of the deep-
>     eddying Ocean
> and yourself go forward into the moldering home
>     of Hades.
>
> (*Odyssey* 10.508–512)

This is the journey Douglas Frame describes as the descent into darkness and death. Persephone is the goddess
of the underworld, consort of the ruler of the dead; the

78

trees stand funereal and deathly, the home of Hades dark and forbidding, associated with decay. Like other descents into the earth, Odysseus's passage carries with it traces of return to the mother's body, of the theme of woman as receptacle or container, as the origin of life and receiver of the dead.

The arrival of Odysseus in the land of the dead is preceded by a description of his journey into darkness. The ship sails, and, the poet says, "all the journeying-ways were darkened." They reach the limit of the earth marked by Ocean, where live the Kimmerians "hidden in fog and cloud, nor does Helios, the radiant / sun, ever break through the dark . . . , but always a glum night is spread over wretched mortals" (11. 14–19). They have passed beyond the realm of the sun, to the zone where the world of living human beings meets that of the dead. When Odysseus sacrifices the animals he has brought, and fills a pit with blood, the souls of the dead come up from Erebos (*hupex Erebeus*).

Odysseus encounters first Elpenor, his companion who died and was left unburied back on Circe's island; next comes his mother, but he will not let her drink the blood and speak until he has heard Teiresias. The prophet tells him all that he must do to achieve his *nostos*, to return to Ithaka, and concludes:

> Death will come to you from the sea, in
> some altogether unwarlike way, and it will end you
> in the ebbing time of a sleek old age. Your people
> about you will be prosperous. All this is true that I
>   tell you.
>
>                                   (11. 134–37)

The word Teiresias uses for true, *nêmertea*, "unerring, infallible," is derived from *hamartanô*, "miss the mark," from which the word *hamartia*, the word Aristotle uses to describe the error of the tragic hero, also comes. The preface *nê* is a stronger form of the privatives *ana-*, *an-*, or *a-*; *a-lêtheia* is similarly constructed. This section of the *Odyssey* echoes with these words for forms of truth, expressed privatively. Teiresias instructs Odysseus further about the behavior of the dead:

> Any one of the perished dead you allow to come up
> to the blood will give you a true [*nêmertes*] answer. . . .
> (11.146–47)

Odysseus, after his interview with the seer Teiresias, speaks with his mother Antikleia, who asks, "My child, how did you come here beneath the fog and the darkness / and still alive?" (155–56). One of the "twice-dead," he will have entered the world of the dead while alive, before he comes to dwell there after his own death. Like Teiresias, who has known what it is to live as both male and female, who has extraordinary knowledge, Odysseus knows both death and life while still living. When the soul of Achilles asks him for news of his son and his father, Odysseus answers:

> As for your beloved son Neoptolemos, I will
> tell you, since you ask me to do it, all the true
>     story.
> (11.506–07)

He says *pasan alêtheiên muthêsomai*, "I will recount all the *a-lêtheia*, all the truth." He comes from the realm of light, of human beings, and knows the unconcealed, the true. The dead know an unfailing, accurate truth, the truth of *nêmertes;* he the still-living hero knows the truth of unconcealment, of unforgetting, of *alêthes.*

Frame describes the associations between *nous*, mind, and *nostos*, return; the man of *nous*, of intelligence, could survive the ordeals of the heroic journey, while the foolish Elpenor and others of Odysseus's companions were fated to perish before their return to their homeland. Frame sees other episodes in the *Odyssey* besides the trip to the land of the dead that exemplify a pattern of return from darkness and death into light and life. The period spent with Kalypso, the entry into the Cyclops' cave, the sleep in Thrinakia all involve some loss and regaining of consciousness. When the Phaiakians escort Odysseus back to Ithaka, and he falls asleep in their swift ship, the poet describes the sleep as death-like, *thanatôi agkhista eoikôs*, "most like death" (13.79–80). Odysseus slept, "forgetting all that he had suffered," *lelasmenos hoss' epeponthei* (13.92). As Frame points out, "One may now observe more closely how the final voyage preserves the connection between *nóos* and the 'return to consciousness.' The last passage . . . suggests that when the hero falls asleep, his *nóos* is removed by *lêthê*."[3] The verb *lanthanô* or *lêthê*, from which *lelasmenos*, "forgetting," comes, is the root of *lêthê*, "forgetting, forgetfulness," after Homer the place of oblivion in the world of the dead, as well as the root of *alêtheia*, "truth."

Dwelling in the lower world brings forgetting which the drinking of blood can only temporarily remedy. Death, the interior space of the earth, place of burial, of the interiority of the female body, the goddess earth, whom the Greeks called "mother of all," represent darkness and oblivion. The very name of the god of the underworld, Hades, *Aidês*, may be an alpha-privative form, from the verb of seeing and knowing, *idein*. His place is that of the unseen and unseeable, like the inside of the earth, like the inside of the body, especially the mysterious cavities of the female body. The hero Odysseus, in the underworld, must use his sword to defend the pit of blood from his own mother, who desires to speak with

---

3. Douglas Frame, *The Myth of Return in Early Greek Epic* (New Haven, 1978), 75.

him, until he hears the prescriptions of the seer, who urges *nous*, an alert and conscious intelligence, upon him in order that he survive the trials of the journey home, the attempts of Kalypso, the "veiler," the "coverer," the "concealer," to keep him hidden though immortal on her island, the attempts of Circe to bury him in the unconsciousness of an animal body, the efforts of the Cyclops to hold him in his dark cave, to bury him in the Cyclops' own body by devouring him, the desire of the Phaiakians to keep him with them in their community outside of history. Odysseus must have *nous* and *alêtheia*, intelligence and unforgetting, to endure.

During the journey of Odysseus to the underworld, while the dead can speak unerringly, the man who moves from light into dark, and then back again, speaks the truth as *alêtheia*.[4] It is the passage itself between life and death, from open, exterior space to enclosed, contained space, that permits access to the truth that is unforgetting. For the early Greeks, it may be the case that—if the female body is analogous to the interior of the earth, the interiority housing the dead and the not-yet-living, receiving the penis like the plow readying the earth for sowing[5]—in such circumstances the woman cannot *know* truth. Perhaps she *is* truth, goddess of unconcealment called *Alêtheia*, representing the fruits of the passage between light and dark without having access to those fruits herself. As such, she is like the slave under torture, the physical space, unknowable, inaccessible to

---

4. Although it may be the case that metrical and formulaic considerations determine the use of particular words for truth in Homeric verse, the appropriateness of a particular word to a particular character may date back to the moment when formulae were first generated, and betray a sense of the various forms of truth to which different characters, in differing relationships to death, have access.

5. See duBois, *Sowing the Body*.

the real subject of truth, yet through which the knower must pass in order to acquire truth, like the slave whose body bears a message that the slave is unable to see, let alone read.

A word used in addition to *alêthês* in the *Odyssey* is *atrekês*, real, genuine, with a connotation perhaps of that which does not distort or deviate. The Latin word *torqueo* means "to twist tightly, to wind or wrap, to subject to torture, especially by the use of the rack." This word may come from the root *trek-*, also occurring in Greek, which may give us *atraktos*, "spindle," and also "arrow."[6] (*Tortor* is used as a cult title of Apollo, "perhaps", according to the *Oxford Latin Dictionary*, "from the quarter at Rome occupied by the torturers.")[7] Our English word "torture" is taken from this Latin root. The *Oxford English Dictionary* defines "torture," an adaptation of the Latin *tortura*, in the following way:

> The infliction of excruciating pain, as practised by cruel tyrants, savages, brigands, etc., from the delight in watching the agony of a victim, in hatred or revenge, or as a means of extortion; spec. *judicial torture*, inflicted by a judicial or quasi-judicial authority, for the purpose of forcing an accused or suspected person to confess, or an unwilling witness to give evidence or information.[8]

Although the writers of the dictionary list first tyrants, savages, and brigands as the agents of torture, the first

---

6. Although LSJ says the derivations of both *atrekês* and *atraktos* are uncertain. For the derivation from *trek-*, see Thomas Cole, "Archaic Truth," *Quaderni Urbinati di Cultura Classica* n.s. 13 (1983), 13.

7. *Oxford Latin Dictionary*, ed. P. G. W. Glare (Oxford, 1982).

8. *The Compact Edition of the Oxford English Dictionary* (Oxford, 1971).

entry in their citations of the use of the word in English refers to the *Acts of the Privy Council* of 1551. This set of connotations, to return to the point, links the English word torture with the twisted, the distorted, and suggests that the truth gained as a confession is in English not conceived of as a straight line, but is rather bent, extorted from time on the rack.

In Greek, however, not passing through Latin into English for our etymology (*etumos* is another word used for "true" in Greek), we have, parallel to *atrekês*, the word *alêtheia* with its suggestion of hiddenness and forgetting. The connotations of the alternative words *nêmertês* and *atrekês* are respectively "not missing the mark", and "not deviating from an existing model"; the weight of *alêthês* rests instead on the trace of something not forgotten, not slipping by unnoticed.[9]

There are other sites in ancient Greek culture that replicate the paradigm of a truth that might be forgotten, buried and inaccessible to all but the privileged seeker. One such is the oracle at Delphi. The consultation of the oracle bears similarities to the voyage of Odysseus to the underworld, the dark place at the edge of the world that provides access to the dead. The presence of the Pythia, the priestess, medium of Apollo's truth at Delphi, marks the former quality of the Delphic site as an earth goddess shrine where a "she-dragon" once guarded a spring, received Typhaon, the parthenogenic offspring produced by Hera as response to Zeus's giving birth to Athena, and was slain by Apollo:

> She brought their day of doom to those who met
>   her,
> until the lord far-shooting Apollon shot her

---

9. Cole, *op.cit.*, 15.

with a mighty arrow; rent with insufferable pains,
she lay panting fiercely and writhing on the
    ground. . . .
. . . Phoibos Apollon boasted;
"Rot now right here on the man-nourishing earth;
you shall not ever again be an evil bane for living
    men, who eat the fruit of the earth that
    nurtures many. . . .
. . . but right here
the black earth and the flaming sun will make
    you rot."
. . . And the holy fury of Helios made her rot away;
hence the place is now called Pytho, and people
call the lord by the name of Pytheios, because on
    that spot
the fury of piercing Helios made the monster rot
    away.[10]

The name of the Pythia, priestess of Pythian Apollo at
Delphi, recalls this origin from the verb *puthô*, "to make
rot, to rot"; that which was dead and should have been
buried within the earth remained on the surface to be
corrupted by the sun's heat. The Pythia sat on her tripod
and received emanations from within the earth that conveyed the message of the god Apollo to the consultant
of the oracle. Her body was the conduit, the necessary
vehicle for the transmission of the divine truth, and in
fact that truth was so mediated, so distorted and mysti-
fied, perhaps by its passage through her body, that frequently it became indecipherable, enigmatic for the
questioner. The Apollonian truth, pure and uncontaminated, after passing through the material body of earth
and woman, takes on a distorting residue of corporeality

---

10. *The Homeric Hymns*, trans. Apostolos N. Athanassakis
(Baltimore, 1976), 25–26.

that separates and distances the divine word from the mortal seeker.[11] As Herakleitos says: "The lord whose oracle is in Delphi neither speaks out nor conceals [*kruptei*], but gives a sign [*sêmainei*]" (fragment 93). The word *sêmainei* demands our attention here because it is sometimes used synonymously with *sphragizô*, "to stamp with a sign or mark, to seal." This metaphor for the relationship between the god, the medium, and the consultant of the oracle bears echoes of the earlier discussion of inscription on the body as a marker of truth, of the contents, the nature of the thing marked. Here the body of the woman is stamped, sealed, with the god's truth; the body itself becomes a sign, with its acoustic rendition of the ineffable divine truth. The consultation of the oracle involves not only the search for the hidden truth, which emerges from inside the earth, but also the passage through the medium of the woman.

Plutarch, in his description of the oracle, says the consultants perceived the message as a perfume that was exhaled from what was called the *adyton*, the "not-to-be-entered," the innermost sanctuary of a temple or sacred site (*Moralia* 438a). The Greek temple, unlike later Christian sacred buildings, presented itself as a significant form in a landscape rather than as an enclosure for worshipers. The altar was frequently outside the temple itself, before the building's main front. The priest who officiated at religious rites usually stood with his back to the temple's face. As J. J. Coulton points out, "Greek architects mainly showed their interest in manipulating space not inside buildings, but outside."[12] Inner spaces,

---

11. For a fascinating study of the Pythia, and her relationship to the Greek notion of virginity, see Giulia Sissa, *Le corps virginal: La virginité en Grèce ancienne* (Paris, 1987).

12. J. J. Coulton, *Greek Architects at Work: Problems of Structure and Design* (London, 1977), 118–19.

the inner sancta, never became public space, but were rather the precinct of the god or goddess and the adepts. The larger temples had a porch before the central inner space containing the figure of the goddess or god, which faced the entrance of the temple. Many contained the *adyton,* a chamber at the temple's back that served as a treasury, inner sanctum, and sometimes as an oracle chamber.[13] This innermost space contained the secret of the temple's treasure, or gave forth the prediction of the future in oracles. This space, the name of which in Greek means "not to be entered, not to have a foot set on it," except that of some privileged functionary of the temple, lies at the furthest remove from the face of the temple, its aspect turned toward the worshipers. As the smallest enclosed unit within a larger system of walls and surrounding columns, it contains the secret at the heart of the temple, a secret inaccessible to *hoi polloi.* This paradigm, of the harboring of secret, inaccessible truth, sheltering it from the many, replicates the order of Odysseus's voyage to the dark edge of the world, even though Odysseus travels to the limits, while the consultant of the oracle moves to the innermost place in the sacred site. In both cases, the truth is inaccessible in daily life, it is something hidden in darkness, something to which only the extraordinary man has access. And if we see the temple as having the form of the female body, enclosing a potential interiority, then in the case of this sacred achitecture the secret is buried within the female form, as it is buried in the earth for Odysseus.[14]

Even in the texts of the Hippocratic tradition, the body is seen to contain secrets that must be interpreted, elicited by signs that emerge onto the body's surface, as the

---

13. See William Bell Dinsmoor, *The Architecture of Ancient Greece* (New York, 1975), 49.

14. See P. duBois, *Sowing the Body.*

emanation from the earth arises to possess the Pythia. In describing an induced miscarriage, this medical writer reveals the Greeks' tendency to observe and theorize about the body, rather than actively to intervene in its functioning:

> A kinswoman of mine owned a very valuable danseuse, whom she employed as a prostitute. It was important that this girl should not become pregnant and thereby lose her value. Now this girl had heard the sort of thing women say to each other—that when a woman is going to conceive, the seed remains inside her and does not fall out. She digested this information, and kept a watch. One day she noticed that the seed had not come out again. She told her mistress, and the story came to me. When I heard it, I told her to jump up and down, touching her buttocks with her heels at each leap. After she had done this no more than seven times, there was a noise, the seed fell out on the ground, and the girl looked at it in great surprise.[15]

The author bases his detailed description of a six-day-old embryo on this incident. The exit of material from inside the body allows him to theorize about its internal processes. The physician does not intervene, but instructs the woman and waits for the body to produce its own signs.

In the treatise called "Prognosis," the author writes almost as if the physician himself were giving an oracle:

> If he [the physician] is able to tell his patients when he visits them not only about their past and present

---

15. "The Seed and the Nature of the Child," in *Hippocratic Writings*, ed. G. E. R. Lloyd, trans. J. Chadwick, W. N. Mann, I. M. Lonie, E. T. Withington (Harmondsworth, 1978), 325–26.

symptoms, but also to tell them what is going to happen, as well as to fill in the details they have omitted, he will increase his reputation as a medical practitioner. . . .

The signs to watch for in acute diseases are as follows. First study the patient's *facies;* whether it has a healthy look and in particular whether it be exactly as it normally is.[16]

The physician must know past, present, and future; he must also be an interpreter of the inner meaning of the outward sign, of the body's truth that is written on the *facies*, on the external aspect of his patient. The movements of the body also bear witness to the internal state and to the future of the patient:

The following points about the gestures of the hands should be noted. In cases of acute fever or of pneumonia and in brain-fever and headache, it is a bad sign and portends death if any of the following things are noted: if the hands are waved in front of the face, or make grabs at the air, or pull the nap off cloth, or pull off bits of wool, or tear pieces of straw out of the wall.[17]

The physician's craft consists in patient observation of appearance and behaviors that reveal the progress of disease within the closed body of the sufferer. He must take careful note of any uncharacteristic gestures, gestures that fall outside the vocabulary of ordinary life, and translate them with an eye to the future. In the Hippocratic oath, the physician must swear not to break the surface of the body: "I will not cut, even for the stone,

------

16. *Hippocratic Writings,* ed. G. E. R. Lloyd (New York, 1978), 170.

17. *Ibid.,* 172.

but I will leave such procedures to the practitioners of that craft." The physician is not a surgeon, but an interpreter of signs, one who uses the outside of the body to know its inside.[18]

Each of these sites of meaning in ancient culture—the epic, oracles, sacred buildings, the medicalized body—lay out a pattern of obscure, hidden truth that must be interpreted. Teiresias must convey to Odysseus the truth of his future, the Pythia is the medium through which Apollo's truth must pass and be interpreted by the priests of Delphi, the temple's outward aspect conceals an inner sanctum, the physician must gaze at the patient's outward appearance and interpret the body's signs, and then predict the future of that body.

These images of interiority are associated in ancient culture with female space, with the containment and potentiality of the female body. And the female is analogous to the slave. The slave's body and the woman's body are marked off as the property of the master; the subject of history in the ancient city, the Greek male citizen, ruled over his subordinates, animals, barbarian slaves, and women, who were seen as like one another in their subordination.[19] Like slave's bodies, tattooed with signs of ownership and origin, women's bodies were metaphorically inscribed by their masters.[20] The veiled citizen woman, who conceals her true nature with cosmetics and drapery, remains an other, full of potential truth, uncannily resembling the slave, male and female, who awaits torture, who conceals truth. While there is a secu-

---

18. *Ibid.*, 67.

19. See Page duBois, *Centaurs and Amazons: Women and the Prehistory of the Great Chain of Being* (Ann Arbor, 1982).

20. See P. duBois, *Sowing the Body*, 130–66.

larization of the meaning of *alêtheia*, as Marcel Detienne has shown, in the classical period of the ancient Greek city, the connotations of *alêtheia*—links with hiddenness, secrecy, female potentiality, the tempting, enclosed interiority of the human body, links with both treasure and death, with the mysteries of the other—persist and coexist with that secularization.

# 9        Some Pre-Socratics

The works of the pre-Socratic philosophers (even to presume to call them philosophers may be to presume too much) present problems of reading for the historian of philosophy, for the literary and cultural critic. Even the problem of who is disciplinarily responsible for these texts is insoluble. And the incompleteness of many pre-Socratic texts causes unease. How can one speak of philosophical development when only one line, one metaphor, one aphorism remains, torn out of context, lines repeated to illustrate a well-known point? The ellipses in the published pre-Socratic fragments recall stopped mouths, messages gone astray, the utter failure of communication across a distance of centuries.

One of the impulses of philology has been to attack the problem of these fragments directly. Classical and biblical scholarship has always been in great part efforts at restoration. Philologists have tried to make whole what was broken—to imagine and guess at the missing parts, to repair what was transmitted inaccurately, to change, excise, add, to return to the original and perfect text of these early thinkers, texts that we will probably never know. The scholars' work has been immensely valuable, in reading, deciphering, presenting to us in legible form much that would be inaccessible without the intervention of centuries of erudition. Their efforts at erudition must continue, as labor over textual mysteries, as supplementation of our ignorance. But until the day of glorious resurrection, when the body of ancient philosophy is miraculously restored in its integrity, what are we to do with the fragments of such a thinker as Herakleitos? Are we to set them aside until they are restored? Are we to continue to long for wholeness, for the truth of the whole?

Recent literary theory has rendered the reading of the fragments of early ancient philosophers more possible, even more pleasurable. It has celebrated the fragmentary. Perhaps because of the rediscovery of Nietzsche, that eccentric philologist, work on contemporary culture has recognized the aesthetic particularity of the fragment. The very search for integrity and indivisibility in all things has been called into question by the heirs of Nietzsche, among them those feminists who see the emphasis on wholeness and integrity, on the full body, as a strategy of scholarship that has traditionally excluded the female, who has been identified as different, heterogeneous, disturbing the integrity of the scholarly body, incomplete in herself. Aristotle describes the female as a "deformed" (*pepêrômenon*) male (*Generation of Animals* 737a), and argues further that her contribution to reproduction lacks a crucial ingredient, the principle of soul (*psukhê*). The project of scientific textual studies has been to supply the text's lack, to reduce the fragmented, partial quality of embodied, material texts, to reject the defective text as it rejects the defective female. Like the slave body that needs the supplement of the *basanos* to produce truth, the female body and the fragmentary text are both constructed as lacking.

The truth of the pre-Socratics is not the truth of integrity, of the monumental wholeness of the text of Homer and Plato. In fact, we now know the monumental Homeric corpus to have its own fragmentariness, not the fragmentation of the Analysts, who wanted to discard parts of the received text as interpolations, but a sedimentation, a complicated series of origins, an unevenness due to its oral composition that prevents it from being what was once considered the seamless, intentional production of an "author." So from the beginning, as we approach the pre-Socratics' work, their aphorisms, bits and pieces recorded in later philosophers, traces of their reputation shaping even in their absence the work of others, we cannot yet—perhaps we can never— achieve a sense of coherence, of systematic development of philosophical ideas, such as is perhaps possible with the works of Kant or Hegel.

I want to approach the notion of truth in the pre-Socratics fragmentarily, then, by looking at truth in the fragmentary remains of the work of Herakleitos and Parmenides, two radically different thinkers. I have not attempted here to present an encyclopedic survey of all occurrences of *alêtheia* in Homer, Hesiod, all the pre-Socratics. Rather, I want to give a sense of a cultural paradigm, of the ways in which the word *alêtheia* works within a semantic field, in its contrasts, for example, with other words for truth, and as it fits into a cultural and social field of seeking out the genuine, the true. Herakleitos seems to offer a suggestive and idiosyncratic notion of truth that has certain affinities with the dialogical practices of the later democracy, while Parmenides' sense of truth is more compatible with the traditions of epic and of the consultation of oracles.

In the matter of truth, Herakleitos says:

Sound thinking (is) a very great virtue, and (practical) wisdom [*sophiê*] (consists in our) saying what is true [*alêthea*] and acting in accordance with (the) real constitution (of things), (by) paying heed (to it).

(Fragment 112)

This kind of *alêtheia* assumes the possibility of a true relationship to the real, *phusis*. It does not posit a journey, a search for truth in secret places. Rather, this truth rewards attention to what is, and is implicated in the practice of daily life. This truth is not estranged from the intelligent conduct of mortal existence, not located elsewhere.

In a tantalizing fragment not bearing directly on the problem of truth, Herakleitos uses the metaphor of torture to describe the practices of physicians:

Doctors, who cut and burn (those who are sick, grievously torturing [*basanizontes*] them in every way), complain that they do not receive an appropriate fee (from the sick) for doing these things.[1]

Although the words in parentheses may not be Herakleitos's own, they appear in the ancient source for fragment 58, Hippolytos's *Refutation of All Heresies*. This fragment has been taken as part of a Heraclitean argument that the same thing can be beneficial and harmful at different times, that the flux of time alters the meaning of such seemingly negative acts as cutting into and burning the human body, rendering them therapeutic when performed by a surgeon.

---

1. Heraclitus, *Fragments, A Text and Translation with a commentary*, ed. and trans. T. M. Robinson (Toronto, 1987), 41.

As Herakleitos says in various and often obscure ways throughout the fragments, opposites are interconnected in a greater unity: "They do not understand how, while differing from itself, (it) is in agreement with itself. (There is) a back-turning connection, like (that) of a bow or lyre" (fr. 51). The *basanos*, touchstone, test, torture, is associated paradoxically with the healing practices of physicians, and there is an underlying connection between injuring and curing.

Elsewhere Herakleitos seems to argue against an innate hierarchy of mortal beings: "War is father of all, and king of all. He renders some gods, others men; he makes some slaves, others free" (fr. 53). Mortal and immortal status depends on human history, on events. There is no essence, no absolute truth in the differences among beings. Circumstances, history, time affect relations of difference and power.[2] This relativism establishes a ground for the vision of equality among citizens in ancient democratic ideology, and even further, a point from which to examine the commonly held view that some human beings are slaves *by nature*.

Herakleitos represents an alternative to the essentializing concept of truth as a buried, hidden substance; he offers a temporal notion of truth, that the *basanos* of the physician is good at one time, at another time bad, that war creates slaves and free, a relative notion of truth. Although he says: "*Phusis* [nature] loves to hide itself" (fr. 123), this remark seems to refer to our need to observe the particulars of our environment with care: "Whatsoever things are objects of sight, hearing, and experience—these things I hold in higher esteem" (fr. 55). Truth can be obtained through attention to the play of difference; the notion of underlying unity is not the

---

2. See C. H. Kahn, *The Art and Thought of Heraclitus* (Cambridge, 1979).

postulating of a buried truth, but a recognition of process and change, of endless movement and particularity in the universe. Herakleitos presents a potential opposition to an aristocratic model of buried truth, of truth concealed and revealed only to the privileged voyager. Even though he frequently expresses contempt for the masses: "The many are bad, only the few are good" (fr. 104), Herakleitos's relationship to time, change and process prefigures values of the democracy and of the pre-Socratic sophists whom the aristocratic philosophical tradition despised: "As they step into the same rivers, different and (still) different waters flow upon them" (fr. 12); "we step and do not step into the same rivers; we are and are not" (fr. 49a). His is not a doctrine of superficial appearance and deep truth, but rather a celebration of the mutability and interdependence of all things. The Heraclitean truth, read within his words, fragmentary as they are, celebrating flux, time, difference, allows for an alternative model to a hidden truth. Even though Herakleitos distinguishes himself from those who do not understand, who lack his grasp of reality, for him truth is process and becoming, obtained through observation, rather than a fixed, divine and immutable truth of eternity.

Herakleitos lived probably from about 540 B.C.E. to about 450 B.C.E. Parmenides was probably born about 515 B.C.E. Parmenides divided his poem, as we can tell from the fragments that remain of it, into two parts, one of which expounds truth, the other the realm of appearances, or seeming. The voice of the poem speaks of having been carried onto the way of the goddess, while the daughters of the Sun, who were hurrying to send him into the light, unveiled their own faces and left the home of night. He passes through the gates of the ways of day and night, guarded by Justice, to be greeted by the goddess on the other side, who says:

It is right that you should learn all things, the un-
shaken heart of well-rounded[3] truth [*alêtheiês*] as well
as the opinions of mortals, in which there is no true
[*alêthês*] belief.[4]

Truth is carefully distinguished from opinion, *doxa*. The
constrast between the realms of darkness and light made
in the *Odyssey* here marks the difference between the
realm of ordinary existence and that of "enlightenment,"
of the goddess' explication of that other difference, between truth and opinion.

The goddess explains her doctrine by saying that "the
one way, that it *is* and cannot not-be, is the path of
persuasion, for it attends upon truth." The word translated "attends upon" is *opêdei*. Alexander Mourelatos
argues, citing the use of the word in Homer and Hesiod,
that "*opêdei* refers to Persuasion's custody of truth, or to
the favor that she bestows on truth." [5] He says further:
"Truth, in adhering to its bond of *pistis* ["persuasion-
compliance"][6], will exercise a compelling power of al-
lurement over men, over each and all."[7]

---

3. In *The Route of Parmenides: A Study of Word, Image and
Argument in the Fragments*, Alexander P. D. Mourelatos makes
an argument for reading the word translated here as "well-
rounded", *eukukleos*, as *eupeitheos*, "persuasive," following
Sextus rather than Simplicius. See *The Route of Parmenides*
(New Haven, 1970), 154–55.

4. G. S. Kirk and J. E. Raven, *The Pre-Socratic Philosophers:
A Critical History with a Selection of Texts* (Cambridge, 1966),
267 (translation modified).

5. *Ibid.*, 159.

6. For Mourelatos's discussion of the translation of the
word *pistis*, see *The Route of Parmenides*, 139–41.

7. *Ibid.*, 160.

In an argument useful for understanding the site of truth in the democratic situation of later Athenian culture, Mourelatos lays out the various aspects of the goddess who reveals truth to the seeker in Parmenides' poem:

The divinity who controls the identity and coherence of the Parmenidean what-is has not three but four faces or hypostases: As *Anagkê,* "Constraint," she holds it "enthralled in bounds" [*en desmoisin peiratos*] and "restrains it all around" [*amphis eergei*]; as *Moira,* "Fate," she applies the "fetters" or "shackles" of its doom or destiny [*epedêsen*]; as *Dikê,* "Justice," she "holds it" [*ekhei*] to its appointed station, without loosening the "shackles"; finally as *Peithô,* "Persuasion," she holds it in the bond of fidelity [*pistios iskhus*] and infuses or endows it [*opêdei*] with the gentle power characteristic of her office. We have in this a complete spectrum from brute force to gentle agreement, from heteronomy to autonomy.[8]

The "what-is," which is truth, or perhaps rather, true, is controlled in these various modes by the goddess, who Mourelatos believes to be, in Parmenides' representation of her revelations, Peitho herself, rather than Justice.[9] In the courts of the later city, truth is figured as the product of torture; the slave is bound by constraint, fettered or shackled, subject to justice, while the citizen juror hears the slave's testimony contained within the persuasive discourse of the litigant.

The word *anagkê,* "constraint," is associated with the

---

8. *Ibid.,* 160.
9. *Ibid.* 161.

yoke of slavery.[10] All of human experience suffers from its subjection to necessity; the slave offers an extreme example of the general human condition. In one of her many forms the goddess who instructs the youth, the *Kouros*, is mistress of "brute force," or of the bonds associated with enslavement, and is therefore binding the "what-is," the "true," in captivity. Like the slave who yields the truth to the torturer, the "what-is" is bound in domination, and delivers up its truth under necessity.

Mourelatos characterizes the difference between truth in the Homeric corpus and in the work of Parmenides in a different manner from that of Detienne. He describes *alêtheia* in Homer as "what happened: the actual, bare, unadorned, unadulterated *facts*."[11] In Homer, *alêtheia* is the reported truth, the account provided by one party to another without distortion. "In the Archaic period another use develops alongside this older use: truth as genuineness, authenticity, or reality—in contrast with dissemblance, concealment, illusion, or appearance."[12] Therefore in the Archaic use of the term, the hearer must always suspect that what is being reported is distorted or misrepresented, that there is a concealedness of the truth.[13]

---

10. Heinz Schreckenberg, *Ananke: Untersuchungen zur Geschichte des Wortgebrauchs, Zetemata* 36 (Munich, 1964).

11. *Ibid.* 63.

12. *Ibid.*

13. Mourelatos points out the confusion produced by what he considers the inaccuracy of Heidegger's translation of *alêtheia* as *Unverborgenheit*, which leads to the English "dis-closure," or "un-conceal*ment*." This translation suggests activity on the part of that which is unconcealed, while Mourelatos contends that *alêtheia* is "non-latency," or "un-conceal*edness*." This more precise rendering of the sense of *a-lêth*-noun-suffix would prevent reading *alêtheia* as a virtual synonym for

The quest of Odysseus for the truth suggests that even in the Homeric universe there must be a journey from light into darkness and back again, that this journey must be undergone for the reporter of truth to be able to deliver that truth, even if he is not distorting the truth when it is finally spoken. Odysseus's reputation and numerous performances as a skilled and ingenious liar cast some doubt on Mourelatos's characterization of the truth in Homer; even though the specific usages of the word *alêtheia* suggest an unmediated access to truth, the insistence of various speakers on the veracity of their speech suggests that the possibility of the lie is ever-present in the text, something that must be fended off in the interaction between speaker and listener. In Homer as in Parmenides, truth is not a simple, transparent matter; it must be won—by the journey, by the effort of the speaker to speak truthfully, to avoid the path of lying that Odysseus takes so easily, the path he often seems to prefer to the way of truth. *Alêtheia*, not Heidegger's shining forth of being, not an effortless radiance of truth, is rather something marked by its emergence from the realm of concealment. The Kouros must travel from darkness into light, must be conveyed by the Sun's daughter, must be chosen for the goddess' instructions, must pass through the gates into the realm of enlightenment to learn the difference between truth and opinion. Achievement of an understanding of truth requires labor, some relationship to *anagkê*, that necessity bound up with slavery; the Kouros must come to terms with the goddess in her manifestation as necessity, in order to grasp how she holds "what-is" in her grip.

Does truth as eternally located elsewhere, either hidden in the body, or hidden in the earth, or hidden inside

---

*phainesthai*, "to shine forth," as it appears in the work of some followers of Heidegger. See Mourelatos, *ibid.*, 64–65.

or beyond human existence, in some realm inaccessible to ordinary consciousness, lead by some tortuous path to the necessity for torture? Can we posit a truth of process and becoming, and another truth of eternity? If so, the word *a-lêtheia* seems to carry buried within *it* support for the view of hidden truth, of truth brought up from the depths. The possibility of forgetting leads to the imagination of a buried realm, the realm of forgetting, of Lethe, which can be represented either positively or negatively. It is good to forget suffering and pain, regrettable to forget a message, to forget crucial information that must be transmitted to a listener; in either case Lethe—or, to coin a word, "letheia"—remains a domain beyond consciousness.

Even though *alêtheia* in Homer may mean accurate reporting, such a notion of truth nonetheless suggests a realm of potential loss; true reporting is a victory, a negating, a depriving of that loss in the name of retrieval of the true. The pre-Socratics' differing relationships to the problem of truth are emblematic of a more articulated difference in the social context of the ancient city in the classical period. Parmenides remains closer than Herakleitos to the archaic view that truth is won by the elite traveler, who journeys to the hidden realm of truth.

*Alêtheia* bears with it the traces of a profound reference, not to be commonsensically distinguished from the other commonly used words for truth. *Lêthê* is a powerful concept, referring not only to the forgetting of pain and suffering but also to the events of life being swallowed up in forgetting, being erased by time, the fate dreaded by the Homeric heroes. *Alêtheia* thus may have reference to the fame of the hero, the truth of history, of accuracy about the events of the past, another realm "elsewhere," another scene. Detienne classifies it in relation to *Lêthê* in the pre-classical period. Thomas Cole's essay on archaic truth argues that *alêtheia* for Homer connotes accuracy, reporting truth without distortion, to be differentiated from other words for truth that refer to another model, or that connote not missing the mark, aiming correctly. The dominance of a notion of truth as *alêtheia*, not forgetting, he attributes in part to the gradual shift to literacy taking place in the fifth and fourth centuries.[14] The legal corpus reflects the state of the problem of truth in the fifth and fourth centuries B.C.E. Charles Segal has discussed eloquently the ways in which growing literacy affects concepts of the self and truth in Greek tragedy.[15]

Cole sets out the semantic field that also contains *nêmertês* and *atrekês*, and Mourelatos supports him in this, asserting that the Homeric view is that *alêtheia* is truth reported, extended in the archaic period to mean genuineness, authenticity, or reality. All who discuss the problem of truth in early Greek thought, in the work of

---

14. Thomas Cole, *op.cit.:* "*Aletheia* is, by origin at any rate, sober, methodical, rational truth" (27). See also Eric Havelock, *The Greek Concept of Justice* (Cambridge, Mass., 1978).

15. "The increasing literacy of the late fifth century, at least in Athens, is one of several interrelated influences that tend to cut the discourse of truth loose from the communal, performative and agonistic context of the archaic period and thereby to require the poet to reflect consciously on the source of truth or, in other words, on the kind of story that he has, implicitly, to tell about himself" (Charles Segal, "Greek Tragedy: Writing, Truth, and the Representation of Self," in *Interpreting Greek Tragedy: Myth, Poetry, Text* [Ithaca, 1986], 80). "As poet-writer who manipulates real bodies in real space on the stage, the dramatist becomes sensitized both to the invisible graphic space of his text and to the hidden, interior space of the self. What is concealed behind doors and gates—the gates of the palace, of the mouth, or of the body—becomes the problem of his writerly art" (99).

Homer and the pre-Socratics, even in Greek tragedy, seem to refer to a notion of truth as something situated elsewhere. The model of reporting suggests a known truth that resides elsewhere, if only in the consciousness of the knower, that must be brought to speech and conveyed by the speaker; at another extreme of this spatial model is the idea of a truth hidden and buried, like the *adyton* within the temple, the oracular truth to be communicated in a state of enthusiasm. Only Herakleitos presents another kind of truth, a truth of temporal difference.

In the dominant literary and philosophical paradigm, the truth is seen to be forgettable, slipping away from notice, buried, inaccessible, then retrieved through an effort of memory, through the invocation of divine possession, through the interrogation by a privileged seeker of some enlightened source; seeking the truth may involve a journey, a passage through a spatial narrative of some sort, a request, a sinking down into the past, into the interiority of memory. This model of truth seeking is consistent with other such paradigms already suggested earlier, in the law courts, where, as we saw, the violence of the torturer is thought to be necessary to enforce the production of truth from the slave, either to force him or her to recall the truth, or to force him or her to speak the truth for the benefit of the court.

The slave's body is thus construed as one of these sites of truth, like the *adyton*, the underworld, the interiority of the woman's body, the elsewhere toward which truth is always slipping, a utopian space allowing a less mediated, more direct access to truth, where the truth is no longer forgotten, slipping away. The *basanos* gives the torturer the power to exact from the other, seen as like an oracular space, like the woman's *hystera*, like the inside of the earth, the realm of Hades, as other and as *therefore* in possession of the truth. The truth is thus always elsewhere, always outside the realm of ordinary human experience, of everyday life, secreted in the earth, in the gods, in the woman, in the slave. To recall it from this other place sometimes requires patience, sometimes payment of gifts, sometimes seduction, sometimes violence.

# 10

# Plato's Truth

Plato returns to the pre-classical notion of the *basanos* as a proof of loyalty and truth; but even more importantly, he presents both a paradigm of truth as recollection, the recalling of time—buried truth—and a paradigm of the production of truth through the *elegkhos*, the philosophical conversation, a version of truth as dialectic, as process, as the making of a truth in time, between people, not as the revelation of something lost in the past but as the production of something in the present. This latter element seems to me the trace of the democratic in Plato, a trace that may be represented only to be disavowed within the larger corpus of Plato's arguments.

But first, let us look at the way in which Plato uses the word *basanos*, which, as you will recall, in the fifth-

and fourth-century legal texts refers to torture.[1] In the *Laws* Kleinias and the Athenian discuss the value of having a test for a lawgiver to apply to the citizens of the city for whom he formulates the law:

> Pray, sir legislator . . . would you be thankful for a touchstone [*basanon*] of the courage or cowardice of your citizens? . . .
> Well then, would you like the touchstone to be safe and applicable without serious risks, or the reverse? . . .
> You would employ it to bring your citizens into such a state of fear and test them under its influence, thus constraining a man to become fearless, by encouragement, precept, and marks of recognition, as well as of disgrace for those who declined to be such as you could have them in all situations? He who shaped himself to this discipline well and manfully would be discharged from the test unscathed, but on him who shaped badly you would lay some penalty?
>
> (*Laws* I 648a–c)[2]

The Athenian argues that this potion, this *basanos*, would provide men with a test for their fellows, and also give a man the opportunity to train himself to face his fears, in a protected environment, away from the public eye. Such a potion would have great utility in the training of citizens. And although he acknowledges that no such magic draught exists, the speaker is preparing in his

---

1. On the *basanos* in Thucydides' history, and especially in Plato's *Gorgias,* see Don Beggs, *Sons of the Dragon's Teeth: Value and Violence in Plato's Dialogues* (unpub. diss., University of California at Santa Cruz, 1987).

2. *The Collected Dialogues of Plato,* ed. Edith Hamilton and Hamilton Cairns (Princeton, 1961)

argument for the introduction of wine as its quotidian equivalent. In defense of the drinking of wine, against its prohibition in Sparta, he remarks that no such touchstone exists, but that wine, in fact, serves to produce the very opposite effects from the ones he has just described, but it could serve nonetheless both as test and training for a young man.

> What can we find more suitable than the sportive touchstone [*basanou*] of the wine cup, provided only that it is employed with a little precaution? For do but consider. Which is the more dangerous course with a sullen and untamed temper—the source of so many crimes—to test it by entering into a business agreement, with the risk of its failure, or by association in a bacchanalian celebration? Or to put the soul of a slave of sex to the test [*basanon*] by entrusting him with our own daughters, son, and wives, and discover his character at the risk to our nearest and dearest? (649e)

This discussion provides a justification of the traditional aristocratic *symposion*, the drinking party. As a test of a man's worth, it exposes his true character, not by making him fearful, as would the imaginary *basanos*, but because it renders him utterly fearless and immodest. His fellows in the symposium, celebrating Dionysos with him, will see the drunken man *in extremis* and will have reliable evidence about how he will behave on the battlefield, in moments of real stress, will perceive the truth of his character in this controlled setting worthy of a corporate recruiter.

Plato's mention here of "being enslaved," *hêttêmenês*, "yielding," "giving way" to the *aphrodisia*, to various sexual pleasures, seems to follow the mention of *basanos* almost unconsciously, as if the metaphor of test/torture required the evocation of another metaphor, that of a man yielding to passion, being bested, defeated by it. To give way to the *aphrodisia* is to exhibit a woeful lack of self-mastery. Michel Foucault, in *The Use of Pleasure,* describes how one of the domains of desire that the philosophical man must master is that of the *aphrodisia;* they provide the opportunity for the exercise of control needed for an admirable existence.[3]

Gregory Vlastos argued, in an early essay, that the paradigm of slavery was crucial to Plato's conceptualizations of psyche and society.[4] Plato uses the metaphor of slavery to understand deviance, the civilized citizen who ought to be in control of his appetites and passions, who ought to use his soul, his *nous,* to dominate desire as the master dominates the slave, but who is incapable of such control. Such a person is enslaved himself, mastered by his desires, in a microcosm of society gone haywire, a fantasy situation that was never allowed to surface even briefly, even in a carnivalesque manner, in Greek antiquity; the Saturnalia, in which Roman slaves played at being masters, was hardly an imaginative possibility in the Greek world. Even though Scythian archers played the role of the Athenian police force, they were slaves of the state, never masquerading as masters.

The Platonic use of the *basanos* refers back in time to the values of the aristocratic Theognidean symposium and the political and social situation of archaic *polis* culture. In fact, in the *Laws,* the Athenian cites Theognis of Megara, saying, "A loyal man, Cyrnus, is worth his weight in gold and silver in the hour of deadly feuds" (630a; Theognis 77–78).

---

3. Michel Foucault, *The Use of Pleasure,* vol. 2 of *The History of Sexuality,* trans. Robert Hurley (New York, 1985).

4. Gregory Vlastos, "Slavery in Plato's Thought," *Platonic Studies* (Princeton, 1973), 147–63. This essay was first published in 1941.

(This metaphor recurs—a thread through this essay, the *basanos* as touchstone of metal, the mention in Aristophanes' *Frogs* of the good old coins being driven out by the bad, later, Heidegger using the metaphor of gold. Does it have to do with the invention of coinage, with the idea of abstract exchange value, and the slave as an exchangeable body, a thing to be tested like a coin, like a marker for exchange? In the *Laws* the Athenian says men are like puppets with strings, and that they should follow the soft, golden string, the "golden and hallowed drawing of judgment which goes by the name of the public law of the city" (644–45).)

In the symposium, on the occasion of male bonding and intellectual and social intercourse, men come to know each other best; theirs is an aristocratic knowledge, one dependent on leisure and luxury. The pleasures of drinking and argument, and the man's conduct on these occasions, expose his character; reliable knowledge of character is not to be obtained in the public debate of the *agora* or of the assembly. In the heat of democratic debate there is a mixture of classes, a promiscuity of talents, the possibility of demogoguery that Plato seems to abhor. Rather than risk this sort of unbridled intercourse, the openness and freedom of public argument, of the persuasive speech that leads to mass action, Plato prefers the symposium, where gentlemen take pleasure together and test each other in the consumption of wine.

The symposium differs from the philosophical conversation, although it has great affinities with it, as we see in Plato's *Symposium*. The *Symposium* records the rather lengthy speeches of particular characters of the Platonic circle, arguments that preserve in some sense the theatrical flavor of the dialogue but that also have the character of brief treatises, of *tours de force*, of *prises de position*, without the constant interplay of debate, exchange, and questioning typical of other dialogues. In the *Laws*, the

Athenian argues the symposium needs a "commander," an *arkhôn*, a master of the occasion, who is both "sober and sagacious," to "conserve the existing friendly relations between the parties" (640c-d). He further argues that such time spent drinking with others constitutes a part of the education of citizens (641b).

Sometimes the Platonic dialogues, perhaps even against Plato's will, preserve a certain democratic practice, to the extent that we find in some of them a mimesis of intellectual exchange. But in fact, for the most part, the characters do not represent the diversity of the democracy, but are members of a certain class. The participant in a dialogue is usually a leisured intellectual, often pederastic in his desires, as are many aristocrats, dominated in conversation by his *arkhôn*, his commander Socrates. Perhaps what we are really seeing is the appropriation of democratic practices, or the *mimêsis* of them, the mask of debate, absolutely controlled and manipulated not only by the master who is the author of the text, but also by a master within the text, one of the participants in the debate who dominates and knows, a subject who not only is supposed to know, but who does know. The text presents not the deconstruction of the situation of master and disciple, but a representation of the inevitability of one man's superiority and natural dominion over others. And the flawed "democracy" of the represented occasion, the pretense of open debate and untrammeled interrogation, is nothing more than the attempt to incorporate and assimilate the seductive techniques of democracy into an effort to discredit it, by this very demonstration of the natural superiority of the few.

The *elegkhos*, "elenchus," the word most often used to describe the process of philosophical dialectic in Plato's work, was first of all a "cross-examining, testing, for purposes of disproof or refutation" (LSJ); it has legal connotations. The Socratic debate in its search for the truth seems somehow to shade, in the practice of the *elegkhos*, into something resembling an interrogation, perhaps even, given the Greek legal practices, interrogation under torture. In the *Sophist*, for example, the *elegkhos* is presented quite pointedly at the beginning as a method superior to a solitary discourse, at least "when the other party to the conversation is tractable and gives no trouble" (217d). *Elegkhos* is cross-examination; the dialogue uses the legal metaphor to describe its own methodology.

The argument proceeds as an attempt to hunt down the Sophist by giving a description of him. Although Socrates does not appear in this dialogue, the "Stranger" serves as commander; in this dialogue, the Stranger's representation of the process in which he and Theaetetus are engaged resembles an account of the chasing down of a criminal, like the hunt for the murderer of Laios in *Oedipus Rex:*

> If . . . we meet with the Sophist at bay, we should arrest him on the royal warrant of reason, report the capture, and hand him over to the sovereign. But if he should find some lurking place among the subdivisions of this art of imitation, we must follow hard upon him, constantly dividing the part that gives him shelter, until he is caught.
>
> *(Sophist* 235b-c)

Although all this imagery is witty and playful, as often in Plato's texts the joke has its sinister side; logic and dialectic are police arts. Philosophy becomes a method of arrest and discipline; philosophical argument is a dividing, a splitting, a fracturing of the logical body, a process that resembles torture.

In the exchanges that follow on this remark, the Stranger uses more techniques of the state's legal power as metaphors for the pursuit of true definition; the accumulation of these images suggests that the conversation with Theaetetus resembles an interrogation, a scene of torture. He cites the argument of Parmenides against the position that "the things that are not are":

> So we have the great man's testimony, and the best way to obtain a confession of the truth may be to put the statement itself to a mild degree of torture [*basanistheis*].
>
> (237b)

The legal language of "testimony," *martureitai*, is pursued in the analogy of the *basanos*, torture; the *logos*, speech or argument of Parmenides will itself be subjected to interrogation.

Here the testing, the torture, is to be enacted not against a specific body, but against the disembodied argument of the absent Parmenides, whose *logos* must withstand this philosophical ordeal. In this sense, the conversation between the Stranger and Theaetetus, his companion in this conversation, resembles an interrogation, a scene of torture. This is a significant move; the violence of the state against the slave has been transferred to the context of the philosophical conversation. Although in the *Laws* the term *basanos* seems to refer to a test in Theognis's sense, some kind of benign testing, the legal language of these passages in the *Sophist* leads the reader to interpret *basanos* as torture.

This dialogue abounds in displaced violence. At one point the Stranger explains to his listeners that Parmenides and others seem to be treating them as children (242c), telling them a story (*muthon*) about what is. He connects the refutation of "father" Parmenides' argument with parricide (*patraloian* 241d). By arguing against Parmenides' philosophical position, and with him the whole Eleatic tradition, the children rebel and commit symbolic parricide. Later, conflict between philosophical schools is characterized as a *gigantomachia*, a mythical battle between the gods and giants which also had its parricidal aspects as an attempt to dethrone Zeus the upstart sovereign, who took over power from his elders, after a series of parricidal episodes. The argument springs up between those who attribute reality only to the embodied, and those who maintain that there are only realities without bodies. "But the bodies of their opponents, and that which is called by them truth [*alêtheian*] they break up into small fragments in their arguments, calling them, not existence, but a kind of generation combined with motion" (246b-c).[5] This imagery of smashing both truth and bodies into bits expresses philosophical opposition with remarkable candor.

Is it the case that the torture of arguments is merely a displacement of torture of the Sophist, and that in part this description of the argument with the Sophist, who is never present in the dialogue, serves to represent him as slavish, as liable to torture and as therefore inferior to the philosopher who dwells in the realms of light? Like the slave, the Sophist yields truth only under violent interrogation and stress. The Stranger, the figure in the dialogue who takes the position of master of the other participant, Theaetetus, continually refers to the sophist as prey, and his interlocutor shares his view of their absent opponent:

> Certainly, sir, what we said at the outset about the Sophist seems true—that he is a hard sort of beast to hunt down. Evidently he possess a whole armory of problems [*problêmatôn*], and every time that he puts one forward to shield him, we have to fight our way through it before we can get at him.
>
> (261a)

---

5. *Sophist*, trans. Harold North Fowler (Cambridge, Mass., 1921).

The word *problêmatôn*, used here punningly, means both a barrier, screen, armor, defense, and something put forward as an excuse or screen, a proposition, a problem in geometry. The metaphor suggests something thrown forward, projecting. The Sophist defends himself physically and argumentatively with his "problems," his armor. Again like the slave's, the Sophist's testimony, without torture, cannot be relied upon. Philosophical debate between the Sophists and the Platonists is represented as a duel, a battle, with arguments serving as metaphorical shields. The Sophist, hunted down like an animal, turns on his pursuers when cornered, brandishing his problems as defenses. But the duel is one-sided; the imagery comes perhaps from war, and more particularly from the hunt, but if the animal's "armor" is his natural defenses, claws, quills, hide, these are inadequate to the assault of human beings' iron, their weaponry.

At the end of the *Sophist*, the Stranger refers to the figure of testing metals, this time obliquely denigrating the sophist by calling him by the name of an inferior substance:

> Let us examine the opinion-imitator as if he were a piece of iron, and see whether he is sound or there is still some seam in him.
>
> (268a)

At least since the time of Hesiod, with his hierarchy of the ages of beings, the first and best being golden, iron suggests baseness, as well as the use of arms in war. The Sophist is a man of the iron age; the *basanos* for gold would be wasted on him. The perfect warrior, a worthy opponent in battle, has perfect armor, a seamless fabric of the finest metals. This opponent cowers, not an equal, a heroic warrior, but a victim. Here the hunting skills reduce the Sophist to the status of an animal.

The *Sophist* presents a fascinating spectacle of violence, parricide, man-hunting, torture and bondage, all conducted playfully alongside the highly sophisticated debate about the Eleatic position rejecting the reality of "what is not." In fact, Plato does conduct an act of philosophical parricide here, perhaps choosing the Eleatic Stranger as master because he has abandoned Socrates as *arkhôn*, as commander of his thought, moved by the arguments of Parmenides and the Eleatics. And the destruction of the position of his predecessors also hints at a desire to wipe out their disciples, their sons, along with them. The text overtly exhibits this desire by thematizing violence, by playing on language that allows a double reading; though it pretends to philosophical objectivity, it recognizes and affirms that what is at stake in argument is the annihilation of one's opponent in the *agôn*. Torture and struggle here become emblematic and enigmatic figures for philosophical labor.

The Platonic dialogues stage not a dialectic, but a hierarchical relationship between a master and a disciple. The tone of the interaction can be flirtatious, matter-of-fact, even sinister, but in any case, the text produces only a mimesis of philosophical conversation, not that conversation itself, and even that fiction of conversation exhibits an absence of dialogue, inventing a scene far distant from the democratic debate of the assembly and the agora in the Athenian *polis*. Democratic techniques of question and exchange are appropriated in the mimesis for purposes of persuasion. The audience, accustomed to the production of truth through argument in the workings of debate in the city, takes pleasure in the theatrical representation of dialogue. The dialogue imitates debate while presenting mastery, the mastery of the philosopher over his student, of the philosopher over the sophist, of the philosopher over the hunted argument. The text finally demonstrates the inadequacy of democratic argument, the way in which a master is always produced in exchange, one participant in dialogue always revealed as superior and dominant over the other(s).

The Platonic dialogues portray not only a scene of interrogation; they also represent a master, a figure of enlightenment, leading and compelling others towards truth as a fixed entity, beyond mortal knowledge, buried deep inside, or residing in the heavenly spheres. In the *Meno*, Socrates has a slave boy recall "truths" he was unaware he possessed, by leading him carefully and slowly through a problem in geometry. The figure of the problem that must be dissolved and unknotted appears in the *Meno* as well as in the *Sophist*. Socrates argues that the boy, who has never before been taught geometry, but who answers questions correctly, must possess truths that were gained in another life. This truth, buried until it is awakened and brought to knowledge, constitutes proof of the immortality of the soul:

> And if the truth about reality is always in our soul, the soul must be immortal, and one must take courage and try to discover—that is, to recollect—what one doesn't happen to know, or, more correctly, remember, at the moment.
>
> (*Meno* 86b)

The scene represents a situation of *alêtheia*, of un-forgetting, of dis-covering a truth gained elsewhere, in another time, almost as if Plato were re-literalizing the two components of the word *alêtheia* for his own purposes. The immortal soul has access to metaphysical truths, acquired perhaps in a vision of the good like that described in the *Phaedrus:*

> Now the reason the souls are fain and eager to behold the plain of Truth [*to alêtheias pedion*], and discover it, lies herein—to wit, that the pasturage that is proper to their noblest part comes from that meadow, and

the plumage by which they are borne aloft is nourished thereby.

(*Phaedrus* 248b-c)

The plain of *Alêtheia* nurtures the souls of human beings, which then can return to mortal life nourished and refreshed by the vision of true being. Mortal existence, which brings the soul back to dwell in the body, obscures that truth to varying degrees, depending on how that soul fared in the realm of the immortals:

> Whatsoever soul has followed in the train of a god, and discerned something of truth [*ti tôn alêthôn*], shall be kept from sorrow until a new revolution shall begin, and if she can do this always, she shall remain always free from hurt. But when she is not able so to follow, and sees none of it, but meeting with some mischance comes to be burdened with a load of forgetfulness [*lêthês*] and wrongdoing, and because of that burden sheds her wings and falls to the earth, then thus runs the law. . . .
>
> (248c)

There follows a description of a hierarchy of mortal lives into which the soul is reborn, its highest rank a seeker after wisdom or beauty, its lowest a tyrant. Life is oblivion of the vision of truth; *Lêthê* is a weight. *Alêtheia* is the forgetting of the body, the forgetting of untruth, the forgetting of forgetting; it is the casting off of the material, deathly, woman-born body, and ascent to the realm of pure soul. *Lêthê* weighs down the soul and causes it once again to be housed in the flesh, in the weighty body, in the untruth and forgetting of the light. In the play in the *Phaedrus* between Lethe and Aletheia, we can see how truth can carry a privative, that *a-lêtheia* is the removal of something, the casting off of the weight of corporeal existence.

*119*

Remembering, dis-covery, is the momentary return to the realm of the winged soul, an escape from the burden of forgetfulness and the body. Socrates says that when a soul is perfect, it stays in the realm above the earth, "but one that has shed its wings sinks down until it can fasten on something solid, and settling there it takes to itself an earthy [*gêinon*] body" (246b-c). The earthiness of the mortal body is associated with the feminine, because of the traditional connection between the goddess of earth, Ge, and the maternal body. This female, earthly body is the source of life, and is also linked with death and burial.[6] Earthliness is the physical equivalent of Lethe, keeping the soul from access to the memory of its vision of true being, before a woman gave it birth, gave it its weighty body.

In the *Sophist*, Plato points out the region of the philosopher's thinking, his emergence out of the darkness of normal human existence into a realm of light:

> The philosopher, whose thoughts constantly dwell upon the nature of reality, is difficult to see because his region is so bright, for the eye of the vulgar cannot endure to keep its gaze fixed on the divine.
>
> (254a-b)

Like the man who dwells in the cave in the *Republic*, the sophist lives in darkness, while the philosopher has entered a divine space of enlightenment.

In the *Republic*, the matter of truth emerges in the allegory of the cave. Here too, as in the *Sophist*, Plato suggests that force might be needed to compel someone to confront the truth, to come to terms with reality. This model of the encounter with truth differs radically from a dialectical, democratic kind of truth seeking, one typi-

---

6. See P. duBois, *Sowing the Body*.

cal of the Athenian *agora* or marketplace, of the assembly of the democratic city, of the exchanges of the sophists themselves. Socrates says, speaking of releasing one of the men bound in the cave:

> When one was freed from his fetters and compelled to stand up suddenly and turn his head around and walk and to lift up his eyes to the light, and in doing all this felt pain. . . .
>
> And if he were compelled to look at the light itself, would not that pain his eyes . . .?
>
> And if, said I, someone should drag him thence by force up the ascent which is rough and steep, and not let him go before he had drawn him out into the light of the sun, do you not think that he would find it painful to be so haled along, and would chafe at it. . . ?
>
> (*Republic* 515c-d)

This passage has been so much read that it is impossible to come to it unmarked by the traces of other readings made of it.[7] I mean merely to point out the resonance here in the forced approach to truth with the model of torture as truth seeking, in that compelling the resident of the cave to see truly involves pain for him, violence on the part of the one who already knows, who must compel the other to move. Of course the compulsion here is directed toward enlightenment, toward the achieving of a recognition of what truly is. The subject comes to know; he or she does not merely produce truth for others. Socrates evokes the situation of the city that condemned him to death, that resisted his questioning, his persistent reminders that its citizens were living an unexamined life. Socrates, the gadfly, the stingray, caused pain in his

---

7. One of the most compelling is Luce Irigaray's, in *Speculum. Of the Other Woman*, trans. Gillian C. Gill (Ithaca, 1985).

interlocutors and some of them put him to death for his trouble.

The Platonic dialogues represent a doubled relation to truth. The truth, however, is located in a particular space, in the mind of the philosopher, the master who controls conversation, or in the past existence, before life, of his interlocutor, in a metaphysical zone beyond the reach of mortal experience. Only relations of force and labor, the coercion through questioning to arrive at truth, the pushing of the young philosopher to the realm of the metaphysical, the power of the master, can enable the achievement of truth, of the philosophical life.

We have for centuries idealized this description of truth seeking. If the exit from the cave in the *Republic* is in some ways an allegory of the Platonic dialogue, of the philosophical conversation that leads to a recognition of the truth, then it is closer to the situation in the *Sophist*, where the *logos* and the philosopher are hunted down, put to the torture, than to the playful flirtation of the *Phaedrus*. But why should we construct our model of discovery as an allegory of force and pain?

# Democracy

**11**

To articulate the past historically does
not mean to recognize it "the way it
really was" (Ranke). It means to seize
hold of a memory as it flashes up at a
moment of danger.—Walter Benjamin,
"Theses on the Philosophy of History"

The ancient democracy must be mapped as an absence. We have only aristocratic, hostile representations of it, from thinkers like Plato, appalled by mob rule, others frightened by the abandonment of traditional religion, by the military excesses of the Athenian people. The *dêmos*, the people themselves, have no voice in history; they exist only figured by others. The democracy is a present absence, something we can never recapture in words or images. It is only an occasion, men standing together in a space set aside for speech, argument, debate, and voting, where the knowledge of one man of another can determine issues of life and death. The achievement in Athens of what Martin Ostwald calls popular sovereignty was hard-won and ephem-

eral.¹ Democracy was rule by the people, process, dialectic—in the assembly of the city, in the city's law
courts. Although it is possible to establish a more nu-
anced picture of this situation, in which the aristocrats
ruled through the powers of eloquence and traditional
authority, in which corruption and bribery tainted the
process and the dialectic, there is nonetheless something
extraordinary working in the Athenian democracy. To
see its difference from the city's traditions, it is necessary
to exaggerate its features, to draw a sharp contrast with
the political situation from which it emerged. It is particular, historically rooted and limited, nontheoretical, absolutely temporal. It is based on the idea of "one man,
one vote," even though there was strenuous debate about
who counted as a man, even though women most certainly never did. How can we know what it was like to
stand in the Athenian assembly, on a dusty, hot day in
425 B.C.E., and argue about what was to be done? But
the living process of democratic debate must be compared, as a counter-institution, to torture and the model
of truth implicit in the traditions of philosophy. Democracy stands as a logical alternative to the written law,
torture, patriarchy, the written, idealist metaphysics,
even though the democracy employed torture, the written law, exemplified patriarchy.

In order to clarify what I mean to represent as an
alternative to the coercive means of the religious, philosophical, othering, torturing mode of seeking truth, it is
necessary to isolate the logic of democracy as opposed
to its historical practice. The logic of democracy, the
notion of equality and equal power among members of
a community, can produce an ever-expanding definition

---

1. Martin Ostwald, *From Popular Sovereignty to the Sovereignty of Law: Law, Society and Politics in Fifth-Century Athens*
(Berkeley, 1986).

of community. The idea of equality has its own dynamic, a pressure towards the consideration of all in view as entitled to the privileges of rule by the people. The reforms of Solon and Kleisthenes, of Ephialtes and Perikles, included economic measures as well as increased citizen participation in political decisions. Such practices as payment for jury duty, for attendance at dramatic festivals, the expenditure of city funds for the ships of the fleet, for architectural projects that benefited citizen workers—all these had the effect of reducing the inequities of wealth among citizens, of pressing the logic of democracy further. Such a notion of democracy required the radical redistribution of wealth, the elimination of social and political hierarchies. For some ancient thinkers, even slavery itself eventually was called into question: Alcidamas, a rhetorician, argued that "god left all men free; nature made no one a slave."[2] Such a logic draws Euripides to a critique of gender relations in his tragedies on women, and brings such sophists as Antiphon to recognize the shared nature of all human beings, slave and free alike.

Such a logic coexists with another, that which bounded the democracy. This logic demands a closed circle, an other, an outside, and creates such an other. And in the case of the Greek city, the democracy itself used torture to establish this boundary, to mark the line between slave and free, and to locate truth outside. It secularized the traditional, ancient practices of worship, of the consultation of oracles, of the journey toward truth, by locating truth in the body of the slave, the other who dwelt so near but needed to be kept so distant in the minds of the free.

There are two kinds of truth competing in the Athenian city. One, a temporal, Heraclitean truth, is produced in

---

2. Schol. on *Rhetoric* 1373b18.

process, in the workings of the city we can only know through their absence, through their presentation in the work of authors hostile to the democracy. This truth is an absent presence, a process that resists representation absolutely. The workings of the democratic polis are visible only in the negative, in their results, in actions taken, in their literary presentation in works like Thucydides' history and Plato's dialogues, which condemn them. This truth has temporality, historicity.

The other truth is the truth of the religious tradition, of a truth beyond or inside, fixed and fixing, constraining human action. This metaphysical truth is Plato's truth, the truth of the soul's vision, of contact with a realm beyond ordinary human experience, beyond the temporality of human life. This is the truth of oracles and, I would argue, is commensurate with the limitation of the democracy to the privileged few. The historical democracy of Athens was a bounded oligarchy, not the ideal of democracy, its logical extrapolation as an inevitable, progressive, gradual extension of rights to all residents of an expanding community. The comic poet Philemon wrote: "Though one is a slave, he has the same flesh; / By nature no one was ever born a slave" (fr. 39); such remarks push the logic of democracy beyond the limits it has attained in historical time. The torture of slaves in the Athenian legal system is consistent with the privileging of oracular truth, like the seeking of truth in the recollection of metaphysical foreknowledge; it denies the production of truth in time and space, producing the other who knows, the philosophical opponent as well as the slave who must be treated with violence so that truth can be dis-covered. Plato represents the symbolic parricide of his antececedents Socrates and Parmenides, as the Athenians practiced the torture of their others, barbarian slaves. Can the violence of philosophical debate be traced to its origin in this culture of violence and torture?

# 12

# Plato and Heidegger

If I understand the pre-Socratics to differ in their relationship to such matters as truth and history, Martin Heidegger sees them as thinkers with an immediate access to being, thinkers deposed and betrayed by Plato. Heidegger calls his essay on Plato's allegory of the cave "Plato's Doctrine of Truth,"[1] and argues that Plato transforms the pre-Socratic philosophers' relationship to truth, substituting for their experience of being's unveiling a modelling of truth as a sort of paradigm, a mental

---

1. Trans. John Barlow, in *Philosophy in the Twentieth Century*, ed. William Barrett and Henry D. Aiken (New York, 1962), 251–70; this is a much modified translation from *Platons Lehre von der Wahrheit. Mit einen Brief uber den "Humanismus* (Bern, 1947), 5–52. Barlow omits much of Heidegger's idiosyncratic translation of Plato's text.

or visual "idea" which thereafter stands between the observer and an appreciation of being. Heidegger says: "What remains unsaid in Plato is a shift in the definition of the essence of truth" (251). Further he says: "What underlies Plato's thinking is a change in the essence of truth, which becomes the hidden law of what he says as a thinker" (257). Heidegger reveals his own investment in the hiddenness of truth here; Plato's "real" truth is not apparent, and must be dis-covered by the modern philosopher.

In an essay on the pre-Socratic Herakleitos, Heidegger mined the Greek word *alêtheia* that we translate as "truth." Heidegger derives the word *alêtheia* from *lantha-nomai*, "I forget," or, as he renders it, "I am—with respect to my relation to something usually unconcealed—concealed from myself."[2] To forget is to be concealed from oneself:

> When we forget, something doesn't just slip away from us. Forgetting itself slips into a concealing, and indeed in such a way that we ourselves, along with our relation to what is forgotten, fall into concealment.
>
> (108)

Like the ancient Greek writers, Heidegger refers to the testing of gold as an example of the search for the true in "The Origin of the Work of Art": "We call not only a proposition true, but also a thing, true gold in contrast with sham gold. True here means genuine, real gold. What does the expression 'real' mean here? To us it is

---

2. Martin Heidegger, "Aletheia (Heraclitus, Fragment B16)," in *Early Greek Thinking*, trans. David Farrell Krell and Frank A. Capuzzi (San Francisco, 1975), 108.

what is in truth."[3] This thematizing of the problem of truth in terms of the baseness or purity of metal recalls the metaphor of the Greek *basanos,* touchstone and torture.

In the essay on Herakleitos, Heidegger further says: "The open is the realm of unconcealment and is governed by disclosure."[4] And: "Unconcealment is the chief characteristic of that which has already come forward into appearance and has left concealment behind." Etymologically, according to Heidegger's analysis, the desire to know, to discover the truth, depends on a model of truth as un-concealment, as un-covering, as drawing something out from secrecy, from darkness. *Secretus* is in Latin the past participle of *secerno,* "to put apart, sever, divide, separate"; *secretus* is "separated, apart;" "out of the way, remote, lonely, solitary"; "hidden, concealed, private." The Greeks' word *alêtheia* similarly connotes some spatial difference, a realm of the covered, dominated by *Lêthê,* by forgetting, and the realm of truth, of emergence into knowledge. I ask, reading Heidegger's essay on the *Republic,* how can the seeker after truth hope to find a truth which is located elsewhere, in another realm, even in the other scene, as Freud called it, except by forcing it out from concealment, uncovering it, lighting or clarifying it, bringing the secret out into the open?

In his essay on Plato's doctrine of truth, Heidegger discusses the four different "abodes" described in the allegory of the cave in the *Republic.* In the first stage, men chained in the cave watch the projected shadows that they consider to be true things; in the second, freed

---

3. Martin Heidegger, "The Origin of the Work of Art," in *Poetry, Language, Thought,* trans. Albert Hofstadter (New York, 1971), 50.

4. "Aletheia," 103.

of their chains, they are still confined to the closed space of the cave. Those things that seemed true at first, the shadows projected on the wall, still seem truer than what appears in the immediate light of the fire within the cave. The freed man is then taken out into the open air where things seem "most true," "truest," what Heidegger calls "the most unhidden," *alêthestata* (259). The freed man's freedom lies in his turning towards this "most-true." The fourth and final stage of the allegory consists of the man's return to the cave, his attempt to persuade those still bound of the truth that lies beyond them, outside, in the light of the sun.

Heidegger describes a progression in this allegory, an approach toward the truth, from a mistaken perception that the shadows constitute the true, to an understanding of the truest true outside the cave that must be communicated to those still bound within. And the language he uses to describe this progression partakes of the violence of Plato's own description: "The unhidden must be torn away from a hiddenness, in a certain sense it must be stolen from such" (260). He holds to his definition of *alêtheia*, alluding to what he finds in the pre-Socratics:

At first truth meant what was wrested from a hiddenness. Truth then is just such a perpetual wrenching-away in this manner of uncovering. Consequently there can be different kinds of hiddenness: enclosing, hoarding, disguising, covering-up, veiling, dissimulation. Because the most extremely unhidden must, according to Plato's "allegory," be wrested from a base and stubborn concealment, even the removal from the cave out into the open of the light of day is therefore a fight for life and death. The fourth stage of the "allegory" gives its own hint that "privation," the constantly wresting extortion of the unhidden, belongs to the essence of truth.

(260–61)

This passage merits close analysis. As so often happens in Heidegger's prose, it is difficult to separate what he himself asserts in his own voice, and what he is attributing to the thinker, the poet, whom he characterizes. But here he is to some extent merged with the Plato he describes, sharing Plato's view of the gradual progression in the approach to the truest truth. According to Heidegger here, the pre-Socratics, in their use of the word *alêtheia*, implicitly use an etymology that considers the search for truth to be an attempt to un-hide, to un-cover it. Heidegger terms this is a "wrenching-away," a word that connotes a certain violence in the pursuit.

The kinds of hiddenness Heidegger lists are particularly resonant in their gender associations, especially given the Greeks' notions of sexual difference. Enclosing: the Greeks sometimes considered the female body to be like a great *pithos*, a jar, as in the allegory of the story of Pandora who, when her body is opened in marriage, lifts the lid from a great jar and releases evils, suffering and disease, into the world.[5] Hoarding: women were the treasurers, the keepers of the household goods, even like the temples holding the images of the gods.[6] Disguising, covering up, veiling, dissimulation: women were the wearers of veils, of cosmetics; even Greek statuary portrays them as covered until very late in the classical period. Women are the creatures of Lethe, of the hidden, of the body that conceals and weighs down the soul.

Heidegger continues to use a diction that suggests violence in the pursuit of truth; in Plato's allegory, truth,

---

5. For all these characterizations of the female, see P. du Bois, *Sowing the Body.*

6. See Helene P. Foley, "'Reverse Similes' and Sex Roles in the *Odyssey,*" *Arethusa* 11, nos. 1, 2 (1978): 7–26; see also Xenophon's *Oikonomikos.*

that is, "the most extremely unhidden," must be "*wrested*" from concealment, in a removal that is "*a fight for life and death.*" The alpha privative of *a-lêtheia* allows for this sense of negation; privation, what Heidegger calls "the constant wresting *extortion* of the unhidden (italics mine)," is of the essence of truth. This language seems to belie the passivity of the knowing subject implicit elsewhere in Heidegger's work, where contemplation of the shining forth of truth, meditation on its radiance, seems to be the behavior advocated and exemplified. It may be that Heidegger here is merely empathizing with the Platonic passage's drive toward truth, and in his empathy sharing its violence; nonetheless he seems to participate with enthusiasm, to elaborate eloquently the necessity for wresting and extortion in this process.

Heidegger used similar language in *Being and Time* when considering the problem of truth:

> Truth (uncoveredness) is something that must always first be wrested from entities. Entities get snatched out of their hiddenness. The factical uncoveredness of anything is always, as it were, a kind of *robbery*. Is it accidental that when the Greeks express themselves as to the essence of truth, they use a *privative* expression—*a-letheia?*[7]

In the cave essay, men themselves are wrested out of untruth, coveredness, and unknowing; here it is things

---

7. Martin Heidegger, *Being and Time*, trans. John Macquarrie and Edward Robinson (New York, 1962), 265. In this chapter on truth, no. 44, "On *Dasein*, Disclosedness, and Truth," Heidegger discusses both Herakleitos and Parmenides. Herakleitos is said to have argued that unhiddenness, *alêtheia*, belongs to *logos* (262); Parmenides shows that Dasein is already both in the truth and in untruth, that there are two pathways, one of uncovering, one of hiding (265).

snatched, robbed out of hiddenness. This understanding of truth differs radically from one based on correspondence, on the adequation of thinking to a thing.

Heidegger makes the point that an allegory of a cave is appropriate when truth is seen as unhiddenness. An understanding of the move from false to true can usefully be allegorized in this way, as a move from the enclosed darkness into the light, when such an understanding depends on a relationship between inside and outside, between concealment and unconcealment. It is here, however, that Heidegger introduces what he finds new and troubling in Plato's view of truth: "another essence of truth besides unhiddenness forces its way into the foreground" (261). In Plato's representation of the attaining of truth, "everything depends upon the shining of the phenomenon and the possibility of its visibleness" (261). Notions of outward appearance, *eidos, idea,* come to the fore. For Plato, the apparent, the idea, is paramount. Unhiddenness is thus attached to perception, to *seeing.* The *idea* becomes the "master of *aletheia,*" and "*aletheia* comes under the yoke of the *idea*" (265).[8] In this shift in the notion of truth, the essence of truth is no longer the unfolding of unhiddenness, but rather resides in the essence of the idea, relinquishing unhiddenness. Truth is correctness of the gaze, not a feature of beings themselves. And this kind of truth, truth as correctness, becomes the dominant paradigm for Western philosophy: "From now on the mold of the essence of truth becomes, as the correctness of representing through an assertion, the standard for all of Western thinking" (266). It is thus that *philosophia* is born, that philosophy later called metaphysics, that philosophy which is "the gazing up at the 'ideas' " (268). The ideas are "the Being of beings

---

8. See also Martin Heidegger, *An Introduction to Metaphysics,* trans. R. Manheim (Garden City, 1961), 154.

which cannot be grasped with the tools of the body"
(268).

I attend with this much care to the Heidegger essay
not because it necessarily explains Plato's view of truth.
It seems to me that Plato, more than Heidegger recognizes, retains much of the ancient view, the religious
view, of the hiddenness of truth. The darkness of the
cave, the cave in the earth, like burial in the woman's
body, is benighted ignorance; emergence, like birth,
allows man access to the sun. Like Odysseus's journey
to the underworld,[9] the time spent in the cave prepares
men for the truth they find in life, and it may matter
little for my purposes whether that unhiddenness must
pass through the ideas, or whether, as Heidegger wishes,
unhiddenness could be experienced directly by the attentive human being, seeing truly without needing the paradigm of the sun.

What is significant about Heidegger's meditation on
Plato's doctrine of truth is first of all his perception of
the essential violence of the quest for truth, the way in
which, in *paideia*, in the education of men, force must be
used, truth must be wrested, extorted from falsehood,
the student must be coerced out of the cave and dragged
into enlightenment. Another passage from *Being and
Time:*

> Dasein's *kind of Being* thus *demands* that any ontologi-
> cal Interpretation which sets itself the goal of exhib-
> iting the phenomena in their primordiality, *should
> capture the Being of this entity, in spite of this entity's*

9. In the myth of Er at the end of Plato's *Republic*, Odysseus
chooses a new life: "And it fell out that the soul of Odysseus
drew the last lot of all and came to make its choice, and, from
memory of its former toils having flung away ambition, went
about for a long time in quest of the life of an ordinary citizen.
. . ." (*Republic* 10.620c)

*own tendency to cover things up*. Existential analysis, therefore, constantly has the character of *doing violence* [*Gewaltsamkeit*], whether to the claims of the everyday interpretation, or to its complacency and its tranquillized obviousness.[10]

This model of the approach to truth perpetuates the paradigm of the torture of slaves, who are constructed as things, entities, in the Athenian democracy, conceives of truth as something hidden, truth seeking as the unhiding of truth, knowledge of the truth as perceiving unhiddenness.

Heidegger's nostalgia for the pre-Socratics, however, in contrast with Plato's allegory of the cave, concerns not this violence, but a meditative appreciation of truth uncovering, discovering, unconcealing itself. Yet Heidegger himself shares in the sense of the truth as something withheld, obscured in daily life, participates in the religious as opposed to the dialogical truth; he perceives and values a truth that hides, that reveals itself only rarely to the enlightened and attentive beholder. It is this kind of truth that resides in oracles, and even in the tortured body, not in democratic debate, in conversation. The truth is elsewhere, and must un-hide itself, or be un-hidden, forced out from secrecy. This paradigm is perhaps not metaphysical in a strict sense, in the way this term is used in the history of philosophy. But it does offer a very different model from that of democratic process; if truth is unhiddenness, it passes from one state to another; it must begin in hiddenness, obscurity, unclarity, and appear to man in its unfolding as truth.

Heidegger's utopian regard for the pre-Socratics' understanding of truth is not an innocent one. His view of the pre-Socratics is in its way as metaphysical as Plato's

---

10. *Being and Time*, 359.

idea of truth. It relies on a notion of truth as "previously" residing elsewhere, since it depends on this truth's appearance as un-folding, dis-covering, un-concealing. He shares Herakleitos's contempt for the many, his desire for meditative attention to the facts of life, without sharing Herakleitos's profound relativism, his delight in infinite difference. How can Heidegger's experience of truth as un-concealment occur without that which Heidegger suppresses, the location of truth's origin elsewhere, in some space inaccessible to man, who waits for the revelation, for the unveiling that is truth? Heidegger discovers his own truth in the work of Herakleitos, who does have a fluid, mutable, temporally unlimited vision of the universe. Heidegger seizes on this view of process, of change, of historicity, but not really to celebrate the temporal specificity of a Heraclitean relationship to truth. He rather sees Herakleitos as one who grasps the appearance of truth, truth in its unveiling, an understanding which seems to falsify the Heraclitean storm of fire, the sense in the fragments that there is only change, only the dialectical transmutation of one thing into its opposite. For Heidegger, Herakleitos like himself is caught up in contemplation of the mystery of truth revealing itself to the rapt witness. Those pre-Socratics who profess another kind of relationship to truth, those who advocate debate, exchange, focus on human interaction, those pre-Socratics called "sophists," in the ancient slur perpetuated in subsequent philosophy—those thinkers do not enter Heidegger's portrait of the golden age before Plato.

Although Heidegger sees Plato as the villain of philosophy, the very inventor of philosophy as technique, as the representation of ideas about truth, as the teaching of correctness of seeing, he shares Plato's view about the difficulty of knowing truth, its hiddenness and inaccessibility, the necessity of force in leading a student towards truth. It is this conviction that truth is located in another space that seems to me compatible with the Athenian practice of torture. In the Athenian legal system truth is considered to reside elsewhere, in the body of the slave. It cannot be arrived at through the process of debate and exchange; the scene in the courtroom, in which defendant and prosecutor speak on their own behalf, cannot be relied upon to provide the truth required for the court's decision. The truth, this *a-lêtheia*, this unforgetting, must be obtained in another scene. That scene is the scene of another exchange, the scene of torture, where the torturer employs not the *logos*, not speech, but his implements of iron. Here the tortured slave receives the attentions of the court, mediated by the body of the torturer, and here he or she is thought to deliver up from the space of forgetting the sought-after prize. The *agôn*, the contest of plaintiff and defendant in the court, is replaced by another *agôn*, that enacted between the city's torturer and the slave implicated in the events of a lawsuit. The metaphysical representation of truth as residing beyond, within, somewhere else, is replicated, produced, reproduced, mimed, in the scene of torture. And it is this ancient, traditional, religious view of truth—contested by democratic process, by selection according to lot, by mass debate in agora and assembly—that anchors philosophical practice, that of many of the pre-Socratics, that of Plato, that of his modern critic Martin Heidegger.

Despite the efforts of many disciples of Heidegger, recent historical scholarship has un-covered, un-veiled, dis-covered the facts of his long membership in the Nazi party. Although it would be inelegant and crude to make too direct a link between Heidegger's nostalgia for pre-Socratic truth, his abiding love of the Greeks, especially in Hölderlin's translation and transmission of them, and his advocacy of Nazi views, we must come to terms with the social commitments of this crucial thinker, who has had immense influence on the work of so many subsequent theorists, including Jacques Derrida, Jacques Lacan, Michel Foucault, and all of their disciples. The fact is that Heidegger was a determinedly antidemocratic thinker, as far from, as hostile to, democracy as was Plato himself. The power of Heidegger's work for many may after all be due to its resonances with mysticism, with ancient religion, with worship of the earth. And it may be that these strands in his work, the appeal to an ancient, unalienated world, to a direct relationship to the earth, a nostalgia, a utopianism rooted in peasant experience, carries with it a model of the body, of gender, of relationship to truth that bears torture with it as an inevitable concomitant.

Victor Farias has assembled some of the evidence concerning Heidegger's career as a Nazi in *Heidegger et le Nazisme*.[11] He points out that Heidegger faithfully paid his dues to the Nazi party until 1945. He was never repudiated by the party, nor did he reject the Nazis. Farias argues that Heidegger supported the radical element of the Nazi party, which was weakened by the defeat of Ernst Röhm and the SA by Adolf Hitler in 1934, but that he remained loyal to the Nazi cause even though he believed the party had betrayed that cause. Farias cites evidence that Heidegger continued to be held in high regard by the Nazis at an important moment in Heidegger's publishing career. The very essay discussed above, "Plato's Doctrine of Truth," was published with Nazi support and active Fascist intervention:

Il faut tenir ... compte de la façon dont a pu être publié le texte sur *Platon et sa théorie de la vérité* dans un recueil édité annuellement par Ernesto Grassi. Mal-

---

11. Victor Farias, *Heidegger et le Nazisme*, trans. Muriam Benarroch and Jean-Baptiste Grasset (Paris, 1987).

gré un veto initial de l'Amt Rosenberg, la publication de l'article de Heidegger fut rendue possible par une intervention directe de Mussolini auprès de Goebbels, en 1943. [12]

Heidegger's Nazism was not an incidental, temporary affair; his philosophical, publishing, academic career was bound up with the theorization of the Third Reich. Farias shows that Heidegger's relative marginalization after his resignation as rector of the university at Fribourg was only relative, and that his difficulties with official policy concerning the university depended on his view that the reforms instituted by the regime were insufficiently radical. Heidegger's views about such crucial matters to his work as the pre-Socratics, *alêtheia*, and the necessity for radical reorientation in education are consistent with his membership in the Nazi party, with his desire to provide a philosophy for the new man, the new society of the German reich. Although we cannot read his work solely in terms of his political commitments to the Nazis, we must nonetheless take account of the absences and the commitments within Heidegger's work that gain resonance when understood in light of his acts, the "social text" within which his philosophical position was generated. His failure to write an ethics is one such absence. Another is his firmly antidemocratic

---

12. *Ibid.* 22. See also the discussions on pages 292–93, 316, 318–28: "Le texte de Martin Heidegger sur Plato s'inscrivait dans le cadre de ce que nous avons appelé sa 'relativisation' du national-socialisme. Heidegger situait ce texte dans la tradition platonicienne pour laquelle la vérité est une adéquation à l'*ens,* et dans une ligne philosophique aboutissant à l'affirmation de l'être des *valeurs.* Il attaquait donc la version déviationniste représentée surtout par Rosenberg, et exigeait en même temps une base nouvelle pour penser le sens du moment politique" (327–28).

stance, visible not only in his love of certain pre-Socratics, but also in *Being and Time.* And the view of *alêtheia* as discovery, as unhiddenness, as revealing, consistent as it is with the ancient practice of slave torture, with a mystical vision of the secret nature of truth, its residence elsewhere, or even its being the revelation itself—all these support an antidemocratic position, a fascination with secrecy and violence.

# 13    Criticism/ Self-Criticism

Remembering the exhibit in modern Rome of torture instruments, I have tried here to recall the tradition to which they belong. I have had to resist lyricizing the tortured body, offering a baroque description of the body on the rack, of the pains of the slave. I have resisted the perverse pleasures associated with sado-masochism and torture, resisted even naming those pleasures as pertaining to the logics of democracy and torture. I have not wanted to sensationalize and exoticize and create desire for torture, to make this text any sort of celebration of torture, a philosophical lure, an antique.

We are all subjects confronting the recent history of fascism, confronting Nazism, the implication of respected scholars and thinkers with the events of the last world war. My interest in torture and in the problem of truth arises in part from my engagement with deconstruction and with its origins in Heidegger's thought. I have sought here to distinguish between an ancient mysticism, which I see continued in Heidegger's work, and democracy, a moment in political process experienced only intermittently in the course of Western history. Of course deconstruction would refuse the possibility of distinguishing clearly between these two entities, would argue that the one is inevitably and inextricably implicated in the positing of the other. The ancient democracy depended on torture; the ancient democrats used torture to know themselves. And I myself cannot keep these logics separate. I have read and loved the work of Heidegger, written this book thinking of him, believing in connections I see between ourselves and the Greeks, fending off imagined objections and stubbornly forging this argument on a tightrope, trying to think through what antiquity can mean for us.

I am dependent on the metaphors for truth in our common language, models of clarification, discovery, invention. Psychoanalysis, for example, the intellectual background of much of our thinking about gender and subjectivity, is a curious mixture of the two logics I have described here. It is the un-covering of the analysand's past, her buried truths, dredged up through memory, given power in part because they come from elsewhere, from a realm outside the quotidian. Yet psychoanalysis is also dialogue, the construction of a truth, the forging of a narrative hetween two people who speak together, not without inequities of power, but who write a new version of the analysand's life in the present. And the scholarly project is a similar search for truth, an interrogation of artifacts selected from an infinite field, a narrative constructed in the present, in writing. What is etymology but the quest for a historical truth, some earlier origin of a word that gives it its present meaning, or contradicts its current meaning and is a truer truth? What I have done here is to look for the origin of truth, the origin of torture, to search in the buried past for the determining instance of ancient Greek torture, to prove that our civilization is based on barbarism.

But memory and writing are production, of course, not merely search and interrogation. And writing is like the dialectic, the production in the present of a present truth. Like democracy, the wrestling with an angel. Memory is production, the activating of traces, the re-membering of something lost. The threat in the labyrinth of re-membering lies in the possibility that there will never be anything else, no stand, no refusal, simply the passive, fascinated examination of how we make meaning. But the political moment is arresting contemplation, the pleasures of memory, in order to act on what is known. As Walter Benjamin said:

> Thinking involves not only the flow of thoughts, but their arrest as well. Where thinking suddenly stops in a configuration pregnant with tensions, it gives that configuration a shock, by which it crystallizes into a monad. A historical materialist approaches a historical subject only where he encounters it as a monad. In this structure he recognizes the sign of a Messianic cessation of happening, or, put differently, a revolutionary chance in the fight for the oppressed past. He takes cognizance of it in order to blast a specific era out of the homogeneous course of history—blasting a specific life out of the era or a specific work out of the lifework.[1]

History is an encounter between the past and the present, a present in which something is at stake. Torture,

---

1. Walter Benjamin, "Theses on the Philosophy of History," in *Illuminations*, ed. Hannah Arendt, trans. Harry Zohn (New York, 1969), 262–63.

democracy, and truth in the ancient world become visible through our recognition of a significant nexus of these things in the present.

Deconstruction has difficulty arresting the slippage between signifiers, stopping the endless play. But there must be an essentialist moment, a moment in which politics and ethics punctuate the infinite flux, some refusal of what is in the name of a utopian possibility. If we say no to torture in the present, in the name of a real democracy, we must at this moment arrest the perpetual motion of difference, recognize our implication in the play of torture and truth while naming a wrong, inside and out, saying now that our complicity with torture must end.

# 14

# Women,
# the Body,
# and
# Torture

Jacques Derrida, in an essay on *Geschlecht* in Heidegger, attempts to account for Heidegger's neglect of the issue of gender.[1] This essay, although written before the worst of the revelations concerning Heidegger's Nazism, belongs to a general apologia for Heidegger, a strategy as it were to rehabilitate or recuperate him for a world in which gender has become a crucial theme for critical thinking. Although my interest in Heidegger's views on gender may seem a detour from the issue of Heidegger's Nazism, it is related; the crudest of Nazi ideology, the scapegoating, the brutality of the extermination of Jews,

---

1. Jacques Derrida, "Geschlecht, différence sexuelle, différence ontologique," in *L'Herne: Martin Heidegger* (Paris, 1983), 419–30.

gays, Communists, gypsies, seem consistent with the locating of difference elsewhere. In the case of Nazi social
policies, the violence enacted against the other involved
torture as well as execution; the belief was not that truth
resided in this other, but rather perhaps that utter falsity
did, that truth would be purified by extermination of the
other. Heidegger's neglect of all these social issues, of
the problem of otherness, is consistent with his disregard
of the matter of "sex," as Derrida calls it, or gender.
Derrida posits a state before gendering, which he identi-
fies with Heidegger's *Dasein*. This essay is significant
not so much for what is says about Heidegger's view of
gender; Derrida has not for me convincingly located a
Heideggerian realm "before" sexual differentiation, a
sort of utopian temporality during which gendering has
not yet occurred, where the division of the sexes has not
yet come into being. Rather, he has pointed to the way
in which Heidegger, like most great philosophers of the
Western tradition, fails to address the question of gender
because it appears irrelevant to the philosophical project. "Man," or Human Being, appears sexually undiffer-
entiated because sexual difference is understood overtly
as a minor bimorphism of living beings, and covertly
because man is man, the masculine being; the female, in
the tradition of Aristotle's description of the production
of sexual difference, constitutes a deformation of the
male, his defective double. The tradition assumes the
normalcy of masculinity, all propositions except those
otherwise noted refer to the norm, the masculine, and
the female is seen as a special case, an exception, important only when issues of a peculiar nature emerge.

The female body—among others—is still represented
as a locus of truth—the site of the hysteric's symptom,
the place of an infinite jouissance beyond the phallus. The
Woman of what Alice Jardine has called "gynesis" troubles the old Truth, while she is reinstated as the signifier

of the true.[2] As Nietzsche says at the beginning of *Beyond Good and Evil*, "Supposing truth is a woman, what then?"[3] Of course there are other others, the Jew, the black, the Communist, the gay man, the lesbian; all of these are exceptions to the rule of the philosophical subject, the Man. And this philosophical subject needs to find truth, needs to locate truth elsewhere in the body of another, employs torture or sexual abuse against the other, because he finds that he does not know truth, because truth has been defined as the secret, as the thing not known, not accessible to consciousness. But there are other ways of describing truth—as the correspondence between words and things, between knowledge and reality, as a multiple, polyvalent assembly of voices. Truth can be understood as a process, a dialectic, less recovery of something hidden or lost, rather a creation in democratic dialogue. Truth that is produced in struggle and debate, the truth of democracy, of difference, need not be imagined as secret, as known only to a few to whom that secret manifests itself. But a hidden truth, one that eludes the subject, must be discovered, uncovered, unveiled, and can always be located in the dark, in the irrational, in the unknown, in the other. And that truth will continue to beckon the torturer, the sexual abuser, who will find in the other—slave, woman, revolutionary—silent or not, secret or not, the receding phantasm of a truth that must be hunted down, extracted, torn out in torture.

Although we may still believe that torture is performed as a means of extracting the names of others, for the old

---

2. Alice Jardine, *Gynesis: Configurations of Woman and Modernity* (Ithaca, 1985).

3. Friedrich Nietzsche, *Beyond Good and Evil: Preface to a Philosophy of the Future*, trans. Walter Kaufmann (New York, 1966), 2.

Greek reasons, those who write about torture in the present argue that torture is no longer performed to obtain truth from a victim. Rather, torturers torture to punish, to offer examples of the pain to be suffered as a consequence of certain actions. They torture to send back out into the world people broken, destroyed, to serve as living warnings. They torture because of their own rage, their own sadistic desire to punish, to offer for themselves the spectacle of conversion, the body of the other so abused that the tortured gives up a belief and thus comforts the torturer who can then himself believe that he has triumphed, that his cause will triumph over resistance. What has this kind of torture to do with truth?

It is important here to distinguish between political torture and sexual abuse, the torture of women and children by men in today's world.[4] The latter seems closer to the paradigm I have been describing throughout this book, the location of truth elsewhere, therefore in the body of the woman or child, and a fascinated, persistent attempt to possess that truth, to control and dominate through physical constraint and violence. The prevalence of this kind of atrocity, in the ordinary crime of the United States of postmodern late capitalism, is in keeping with the tradition of truth seeking and torture of the Western philosophical tradition.[5] And of course,

---

4.  Elaine Scarry warns against the metaphorical use of the word *torture* in everyday life, in *The Body in Pain: The Making and Unmaking of the World* (Oxford, 1985). See especially chapter 1, "The Structure of Torture: The Conversion of Real Pain into the Fiction of Power," pp. 27–59. This is an important and powerful book. I differ from it in not believing in the ahistorical categories of creation, world, civilization, which Scarry posits as the entities undone by torture.

5. On philosophy and torture, see William Twining and Barrie Paskins, "Torture and Philosophy," in *The Aristotelian Society*, supp. vol. 52 (Tisbury, Wilts., 1978), 143–94.

many of those tortured by torturers elsewhere in the world, in so-called political torture, are women; some of the most horrifying stories to emerge from Argentina concern the torture and violation of women's bodies.[6] Here in the United States, in England and in Europe, however, what I have been calling torture seems to apply more to the abuse of women, those crimes of torture committed by isolated and psychotic men. I would link these crimes to traditional misogyny, which has in recent theorical writing been buttressed by what I see as a Heideggerian strain in critical theory, one that rejoices in mystery, in the secret. This is perhaps one way of understanding what Alice Jardine has called "gynesis," the setting of women at the margin of comprehensibility in the work of such thinkers as Jacques Lacan, where they stand before, beyond, outside the law of the phallus, that is, somehow in a realm of truth. The psychotic pursues women's truth through torture.

Such practices differ from torture of the political variety, revealed in narratives depicting appalling cruelty and the most cynical disavowal of the rights of others exemplified by the state torturers, the political party torturers, of many parts of the global nation in the present day. A principal motive of torture of this sort is control, the domination of an unpalatable truth. That truth may be communism, nationalism, democracy, any number of threatening political beliefs that disrupt the unity, the unblemished purity and wholeness of the state, or of any entity analogous to the unitary philosophical subject. The truth is something else, something missing, either a supplement, the rest which is lacking to the subject, or that extra which threatens to undo it, which

---

6. See the recent work of Jean Franco, for instance "Self-Destructing Heroines," *The Minnesota Review* ns 22 (1984), 105–15.

added onto it will overturn it.[7] This truth, located in the body of the revolutionary, the student, the dissident, must be rooted out, extracted and dominated, in the process of torture. Torture flourishes in intolerance of difference, inability to permit democratic exchange— that complication, negotiation, the flash of real democracy, of Tien An Men Square, a space like the Athenian assembly.

In one of the more compelling accounts of torture in contemporary fiction, Marguerite Duras returns to the ancient model of torture as discovery. Her text reverses the traditional doublet of male torturer, female victim; the scene represents nonetheless a moment of discovery, in which the female interrogator encounters her own sadism. In *La douleur* she describes an incident in which an informer is beaten by members of the Resistance; although those torturing him already know him to be a *donneur*, an informant, they pummel him until he confesses that he possessed a green card, the sign of the German secret police. While her male colleagues beat him, the woman Thérèse interrogates him:

> Il faut frapper. Ecraser. Faire voler en pièces le mensonge. Ce silence ignoble. Inonder de lumière. Extraire cette vérité que ce salaud-là a dans la gorge. La vérité, la justice. Pour quoi faire? Le tuer? A qui ça sert? Ce n'est pas pour lui. Ça ne le regarde pas. C'est pour savoir. Taper dessus jusqu'à ce qu'il éjacule sa vérité, sa pudeur, sa peur, le secret de ce qui le faisait hier tout puissant, inaccessible, intouchable.[8]

---

7. Torture in this sense resembles scholarship, the hunt for a last elusive bit of evidence in some archive, a crucial footnote that will finally decide the case.

8. Marguerite Duras, *La douleur* (Paris, 1985), 155. "It is necessary to strike. To crush. To make the lie fly into pieces. This ignoble silence. To flood it with light. To extract that

Elsewhere Duras calls this process an *accouchement*," a giving birth (160). She insists on the truth seeking behind the torture, although the passage above suggests that there is also a desire for revenge against this man who had been all-powerful. But even this becomes a search for truth, for the secret which made him so. The ancient *topoi*, the darkness and silence of the hidden truth, return in Duras's representation of twentieth-century torture. Duras seems to revel in the hardness, the imperturbability of the female interrogator. If she is ironic, critiquing the logic that depicts truth as a hidden secret, she nonetheless expresses a characteristically voyeuristic pleasure at the spectacle of this beating. Duras seems fascinated with her own sadism, with some putative heightened authenticity emerging out of violence. She writes:

> Elle sent pour la première fois que dans le corps de l'homme il y a des épaisseurs presque impossibles à crever. Des couches et des couches de vérités profondes, difficiles à atteindre. . . . Il faut tenir, tenir. Et tout à l'heure sortira, sortira toute petite, sortira dure comme un grain la vérité.[9]

---

truth which this shit has in his throat. Truth, justice. To do what? To kill him? Whom would that help? It's not for him. That has nothing to do with him. It's to know. To beat on him until he ejaculates his truth, his shame, his fear, the secret of what made him yesterday all-powerful, inaccessible, untouchable."

9. *Ibid.*, 156. "She feels for the first time that in the man's body there are densities almost impossible to break through. Layers and layers of profound truths, difficult to get to. . . It is necessary to hold on, hold on. And presently will come out, will come out, a tiny thing, will come out hard like a seed, the truth."

For this writer the process of torture takes on the metaphorical language of reproduction; truth is born from
torture, it is released in a painful labor that turns the
informer into a woman giving birth. The victim of torture is feminized in the process of torture, or rather made
androgynous, since the production of truth resembles an
ejaculation as much as a giving birth. Like the pear made
to be inserted in the womb, in the Quirinale exhibit
of torture instruments, like the Iron Maiden miming
pregnancy, the violence of this interrogation scene
evokes the reproduction of truth.

While it may be the case that torture in the world
today is still sometimes directed toward the discovery
of truth, in the sense that it attempts to hunt down and
eradicate truths that threaten the stability of certain
regimes, perhaps Sartre's observation that torture seeks
to create an other is the more useful distinction here.[10]
Most of those who write about torture in the present day
are convinced that contemporary torture is not aimed
at producing truth, not an exercise in the gaining of
information. Edward Peters, for example, in his important book *Torture*, says: "It is not primarily the victim's
information, but the victim, that torture seeks to win—
or reduce to powerlessness."[11]

As my discussion of ancient Greek torture stressed, the
desire to create an other and the desire to extract truth
are inseparable, in that the other, because she or he is
an other, is constituted as a source of truth. But the
emphasis on one or the other aspect of this process may
have shifted. Torture in Nazi-occupied Paris, in Algeria
in Sartre's day, or in El Salvador in the 1980s, South

---

10. On resistance to torture, imprisonment and oppression,
see Barbara Harlow, *Resistance Literature* (New York and London, 1987).

11. Edward Peters, *Torture* (Oxford, 1985), 164.

Africa in the 1990s, creates what Sartre calls another "race," a species that is rendered, by the activity of the torturer, not-human. The tortured human being may be black, Communist, revolutionary, gay, but the torture reduces the particularity of difference, of otherness, to that fact of being tortured. All those tortured are "othered," made slaves to the torturer-master. This is what we might call the internal meaning of the dialogue between torturer and tortured, the hierarchical identities established between the one and the other.

The external meaning of torture in the present takes on a different sense when considered in relation to the external meaning of slave torture in the ancient world. And it is perhaps for this reason that the inquiry into torture in antiquity has significance, in that it reveals how this physical act, the deliberate and systematic infliction of pain on another human being, what we call torture, changes in its social meaning over time. Torture in the present, besides being an attempt to intimidate personally those inclined to resist some particular political policy, has meaning as social display. In this sense it refutes Michel Foucault's argument in *Discipline and Punish* that displays like that of the execution of the regicide Damiens belong to the past, that they are part of the *ancien régime*, that we are all so thoroughly disciplined now, have so deeply internalized our own policing, that we no longer need the spectacle of punishment.[12] The chronological sequence of Foucault's book suggests that "Torture," discussed in part 1 (3–69), was replaced first by "Punishment" (73–131), and finally by "Discipline" (135–308), the panopticism of the carceral system and its internalization in modern bodies. Foucault says, after citing an 1836 plan for an improved

---

12. Michel Foucault, *Discipline and Punish: The Birth of the Prison*, trans. Alan Sheridan (New York, 1979).

Paris, where hospitals, almshouses, madhouses, and prisons are grouped together, surrounded by wardens and governmental bodies, "We are now far away from the country of tortures, dotted with wheels, gibbets, gallows, pillories" (307). Tell it to the El Salvadorans.

This argument is resolutely Eurocentric. Foucault's description of the transition from spectacular torture and execution to internalized discipline remains a local analysis. At the same time that the English cease to indulge in public execution, they continue to deport criminals to distant lands, to displace the violence of spectacle elsewhere in the world without relinquishing it. Foucault's account of the process he describes must be faulted for its limited validity; it loses its imperative quality when considered in light of colonialism, the exportation of control through violence, the global economy. France is not free of torture, not committed to discipline, if the French regime in Algeria is engaging systematically in torture, torture of Algerians that was perhaps imported into metropolitan France as well. Torture in the formerly colonized world is not merely another fact in the world, to be set alongside its absence in the colonizing world; these two facts should be related to each other and explained in terms of one another. Moreover, one suspects that the forms of torture in postcolonial societies are closer to the forms introduced by the colonizers than to those of indigenous cultures. Are we to understand that El Salvador is merely a barbaric, insufficiently evolved, underdeveloped nation that is undergoing its medieval phase, on the path to discipline? This view seems to me seriously to underestimate the ways in which we inhabit a global economy of punishment and discipline, in which neither France nor Algeria, for example, can be understood in isolation from one another. If torture is no longer systematically carried out in the metropolis, if the FBI does not indulge in torture, surely the displacement of torture into the third world, the training and funding of torturers by North Americans, must be taken into account in any history of torture.

And it may be that the function of torture today, rather than the production of truth, is still one of spectacle, of the production of broken bodies and psyches, both for local and international consumption. Those tortured in El Salvador are seen and recognized by El Salvadorans; they are also brought to centers in Denmark, the United States, and elsewhere for rehabilitation. They bear witness to the suffering inflicted by agents of the United States, the torturers of the infamous SAVAK, for example, who tortured for the Shah of Iran, ally of several American governments. They comfort American liberals who rest contented in their view that such things could never happen here. They confirm the perspective from the United States and Europe that barbarism resides elsewhere, in the other, that other world, unenlightened, steeped in medievalism and bloody cruelty.

As an article in *U.S. News and World Report* recounts:

Torture has been practiced in 98 countries during this decade, by Amnesty International's count. Contrary to popular imagination, its primary use today is not to gain information. It is a tool for political repression, used to mentally destroy people in captivity, then release them to strike terror into the community. The more extreme the pain and torment, the more horrifying the message and the easier it becomes to intimidate a dissenting population.[13]

What is most striking about this article is its self-congratulatory tone. The United States is a refuge for the

---

13. Michael Satchell, "For ultimate survivors, a place to heal," *U.S. News and World Report*, Dec. 19, 1988, 38.

tortured, a place of healing. And of course it is that, of course the humanitarian work of such places as the Minneapolis Center for Victims of Torture is invaluable, even though its workers, like others in this field, fear that their published research may be helping torturers elsewhere refine and polish their techniques. But what is frequently missing from horrified accounts of torture in the world is a critical assessment of the United States' part in the proliferation of torture in that world, its support of regimes that routinely employ torture as a matter of legal and political policy, or that tolerate or use illegal death and torture squads to enforce public order. Augusto Pinochet of Chile, Argentina's Jorge Rafael Videla and Leopoldo Galtieri, Gustavo Alvarez of Honduras were all trained at the United States Army's School of the Americas in the Panama Canal Zone and at its analogue in the U.S., in Fort Benning, Georgia. Classes included "Interrogation by Military Intelligence."[14] This is not to suggest that Latin American fascists are not perfectly capable of devising and implementing methods of torture quite independently of the United States, but rather that the attitude of pious horror on the part of the mainstream press when confronted with third world torture seems disingenuous.

Perhaps this is the most important observation to be made—to point to the way in which torture is no longer only a relationship between the torturer and tortured, a

---

14. See Lawrence Weschler, "The Great Exception," *The New Yorker* April 3, 1989, 48. On another dimension of truth in relation to torture, the disposition of torturers by the justice system after the regimes of torturers are overturned: "If anything, the desire for truth is often more urgently felt by the victims of torture than the desire for justice. People don't necessarily insist that the former torturers go to jail— there has been enough of jail—but they do want to see the truth established" (43).

local matter of the discovery of truth, of the creation of an other in whom truth resides, from whom truth can be extracted. Rather torture has become a global spectacle, a comfort to the so-called civilized nations, persuading them of their commitment to humanitarian values, revealing to them the continued barbarism of the other world, a world that continues to need the guidance of Europe and North America, a guidance that is offered in the form of a transnational global economy controlling torture as one of the instruments of world domination.[15] And the ancient model of truth, and slave torture as the extraction of truth, still defines the first world's relationship to third world torture. While the suffering of revolutionaries under the regimes of torturers punishes and controls the citizens of their nations, the citizens of the first world observe and deplore the spectacle of third world primitivism and barbarism. The first world contents itself with other ways of achieving truth—the so-called pluralism of mass consumerism, the "freedom" capitalism offers to choose among an assortment of putative truths as one chooses among alternate toothpastes. The truth is that torture still exists, it has not been eliminated in a surge of enlightened globalism, and the third world, in its complexity, multiplicity, multiple sites, has become, besides the site of torture, the spectacle of the other tortured for us.

---

15. See for example the case of the American police instructor Daniel Mitrione, sent to Uruguay by the Agency for International Development. As Lawrence Weschler points out, "In Montevideo today it is hard to find anyone who doubts that he was in fact doing exactly what the Tupamaros said he was doing: training the Uruguayan police in techniques of 'precise' and 'efficient' torture for use during interrogation" (*ibid.*, 46). Mitrione was subsequently executed by the Tupamaros. See also Pierre Vidal-Naquet, *Torture: cancer of democracy*, trans. B. Richard (Baltimore, 1963).

# Index

Printed in Great Britain
by Amazon